"As I read Carolyn Helsel's important r̶ communities, I kept repeating the same thing: 'Wow. That chapter alone was worth the price of the book!' I felt that for the Prologue, and again with the list of myths in chapter 3, then again with the summary of racial identity theory in chapter 4, and . . . basically, with every chapter in the book. Helsel gets what so many preachers — and the predominantly white congregations they serve — so desperately need in these critical times."
  — Brian D. McLaren, author/speaker/activist

"Helsel provides an indispensable guide to help white preachers re-translate the Christian story in light of the biblical, theological, and historical research of scholars of color. This book is not a primer on preaching about racism: rather it shows you how to center everyday anti-racist practices into your weekly sermon preparation. Becoming anti-racist is ongoing work, and Helsel cares for the reader without sacrificing her prophetic claim that to follow the way of Jesus is to take part in dismantling racism in the United States today."
  — Dori Baker, Forum for Theological Exploration

"If you want your faith community to keep or regain a truly credible public testimony, read this book. Carolyn Helsel lays out a straightforward imperative for preaching about racism and leading congregations in ways that counteract the poisonous effects of white supremacist assumptions. The book provides the guidance we need to face an often daunting task. Our current historical moment provides the urgency for this kind of prophetic leadership. May God provide us the courage to follow through."
  — Matthew L. Skinner, Luther Seminary, and cohost of *Sermon Brainwave*

"Despite frequent discourses on race/racism and the awareness of its tragic history in our country, the lack of knowledge among Euro-Americans about the roots and manifestations of racist ideology in our society is shocking. This lack of awareness is prevalent on many levels, including individual, political, and institutional. Racism in the church has devastating effects upon its victims, as well as upon church ministries. Carolyn B. Helsel is courageous and prophetic in tackling such a controversial subject. . . . It is incumbent upon faith leaders to preach on issues of race and racism in genuine and practical ways if we are to reach our congregants. Toward this goal the book is a must-read."

— Samuel Cruz, Union Theological Seminary

"As a pastor, professor, and preacher this book gives me courage, strength, and a determination to preach to the dried-up bones we call the church. It is my prayer that faith leaders will find here in this book fresh hints of God's unfolding future, along with a charge and challenge to confront the great issue of our time: racism. Carolyn Helsel has masterfully crafted a book that engages today's preacher and allows us to find our own voice in the pulpit. I find this book a hope-filled account of God's unwillingness to give up on God's preacher and Christ's Church. This work of homiletical art should be read and consumed by all."

— Robert W. Lee IV, Appalachian State University, and author of
    A Sin by Any Other Name

"Perhaps no subject is as fraught for the preacher as race. And yet perhaps no subject is as vital for churches to grapple with theologically today. Helsel expertly guides preachers and communities into a homiletical imagination that can help transform these communities by centering and embracing the good news that Jesus has delivered us from the multifold sins of racial superiority. Eschewing facile calls to unity masquerading as privilege while embracing the complexities of the witness of scripture, theology, and proclamation, Helsel is both unflinching about the need for such transformative preaching and honest about its challenges. In this way, she offers preachers and laypeople alike a path toward the kind of repair our world yearns for most today."

— Eric Barreto, Princeton Theological Seminary, and coeditor of
    Reading Acts in the Discourses of Masculinity and Politics

PREACHING ABOUT

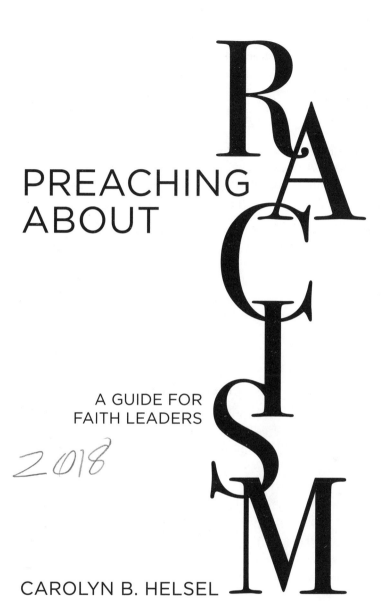

RACISM

A GUIDE FOR FAITH LEADERS

2018

CAROLYN B. HELSEL

chalice press

Saint Louis, Missouri

An imprint of Christian Board of Publication

ChalicePress.com

Print: 9780827231627
EPUB: 9780827231634
EPDF: 9780827231641

Printed in the United States of America

Contents

Prologue

A Quick Guide for Busy Religious Professionals

You're busy. I know. Meetings to attend, people to visit in hospital rooms, a sermon or message to write. The relentless coming of holy days when your community of faith expects you to have a word ready. Expectations on you to inspire. To bring glory to God. To proclaim a word from God to the people. To bring hope. To make meaning of the most recent tragedy or international crisis. To call people to action. To calm fears. To evoke gratitude and kindness. To point listeners to the neighbors in our midst, the neighbors across town, the neighbors of our own faith tradition, as well as those of other faiths, the neighbors around the world who we are called to love as we love ourselves.

You have a lot to think about, and heavy thoughts weighing you down. Your call to ministry is a call to do hard things, and preaching is one of them. I do not want to add another heavy load to your burden. I know the concerns that make your job challenging enough as it is.

However, there is another challenge that has nagged you in the back of your mind that you may not give voice to very often. It goes by different names, though it tends to lurk in the background, trying to go unnoticed. Some call it "bias," others "racism," perhaps "white privilege," —even "white supremacy." It may be stated as a demographic observation: "*predominantly* white." Or, "segregation." It shows up in the form of white nationalism rallies, and also in political language about immigration. It appears in discussions of criminal justice: racial profiling and police brutality, practices of "stop and frisk," the "school-to-prison-pipeline," and mass incarceration. In some communities, there is talk of racial reconciliation. In others, an insistence that reconciliation cannot happen without reparations. Or, in some communities, where whites are becoming the racial minority, there is growing fear and resentment on the part of whites toward nonwhites they see "taking their jobs." And with that, a door in your mind shuts. Your brain closes off this nagging idea that is too complicated and too divisive.

If you are white, there may be times when racism remains utterly hidden from your consciousness. However, that is starting to change. That is why you are reading this book. You have a lot of other things

1

to attend to, but you have chosen to pick up this book and read what it has to say—because you are sensing that this is something you need to understand, that needs to be part of your own spiritual growth, that you need to incorporate into your preaching in order to be faithful in your own calling.

As a white Christian, as a preacher, and as a professor of preaching, I have been thinking about this issue for more than 10 years, and I spent several of those years in full-time studies to try and come up with ways to help other preachers like myself be able to preach about racism in white congregations. My journey began in seminary when I first awakened to the reality of racism, and I felt ashamed that my Christian upbringing in white communities had sheltered me from this reality. It was also a stressful part of our country's history: I began seminary in the fall of 2001, with the terrorist attacks of September 11, 2001 occurring only an hour away from my seminary. In the aftermath of our national grief and shock, Muslim Americans and other citizens of Arab descent became targets of hate crimes and new forms of racism. After seminary I worked on the U.S.-Mexico border as a hospital chaplain and witnessed firsthand the deadly risks persons take to seek refuge in this country. A year later I was ordained to serve in a church that was home to many military families, with members being called away to serve in the new wars in Afghanistan and Iraq. Over these years, in the news and in my reading, I saw the complicated intersections of race with militarism, our national debates on immigration, and the fear of strangers, but I struggled with how to talk about it without offending these men and women who had made significant sacrifices already for their country and who continued to serve their community with loving faithfulness. Add to this the fact that from my own experience, talking about racism was always uncomfortable and made me feel ashamed. How could I preach about racism in predominantly white congregations without simply making listeners feel ashamed or guilty?

I answered that question through returning to school and getting a Ph.D., but then I had to re-translate what I had learned from an academic tone to one in which I could communicate to an audience broader than the five people who read my dissertation. My first book, *Anxious to Talk about It: Helping White Christians Talk Faithfully about Racism*, was written for people in the church. I tried my best to write without academic jargon and from my heart, modeling a kind of dialogue that can build relationships with people across different backgrounds. In *this* book, written for you, fellow preachers and religious leaders, I still will be writing from my heart; I also will be bringing to the forefront some of the theoretical foundations I have found most helpful in framing my own preaching and teaching about the subject to others.

I also want to broaden the audience: I write not only to other white Christian leaders, but to *all* faith leaders. After publishing my first book, I heard from members of other faith communities who said: "Why is your book just for Christians? People in my faith tradition need to talk about this too." Communities of faith are locations ripe for compassionate service. White Christians are not the only people wanting to learn more about how to have these conversations. People of color read my first book and participated in workshops I led, and they told me they needed ways for talking about racism too. Persons of faith of all colors who have identified that racism is a problem in our society want tools for talking about racism in their own communities. I write as a Christian with a particular view of scripture and theological perspective, and so I know that not all Christians will agree with everything I offer here, but I hope if you are reading this from another perspective, you can make use of what you find here in your own context.

Knowing how busy you are caring for your community, I have made summary suggestions at the end of each chapter, enabling you to pick up this book when you have time and gain some ideas for preparing thoughtful and sensitive sermons or messages on this important subject. I also have included references and footnotes in this book so that you have other resources to turn to when you want to learn more and suggest studies for your worship community. My last chapter focuses on the process of preparing talks and ways you can work beyond the pulpit or lectern to engage your congregation in the hard work of addressing, understanding, and taking action against racism. My main goal is to make it as easy as possible for you to talk about this truly difficult subject in your congregation. I hope you agree we need as many people as possible talking about this and trying to find ways to work together in the world today.

Responding to Questions about This Work

To navigate the potential objections to preaching about racism, you'll want to be prepared with responses to the following common questions.

1. Aren't you perpetuating racism by talking about race? Why do we have to make such a big deal about it? It will go away if we stop bringing it up!

Racism *IS* a big deal, a bigger deal than we would like to believe. Not talking about race and racism has been a strategy our society has used in the past, but it has not worked. People continue to have biases that they act on, with the biggest impact falling upon communities of color.

If religious leaders do not talk about it, and if our congregants are not able to talk about it, our biases will continue to harm others. Also, by not talking about it, we are discounting the stories of men and women of color who experience their race as having a daily impact on their lives. If we do not talk about it, it feels as if we are ignoring their pain. As people of faith, we are all called to attend to the suffering of one another. In order to attend to this suffering, we need to first acknowledge that it exists. Racism continues to exist, and refusing to name it will not make it go away.

2. Shouldn't people of color be the ones to bring up this subject?

This question addresses my own racial position as white. Since I do not experience racial discrimination, how can I talk about racism? Here is how I answer: Racism began with white people using it to justify enslaving African peoples, and it was white Christians who argued for slavery on biblical grounds. White people as a group continue to benefit unfairly from a racist system. This is why white people need to take responsibility to do our own work, to learn about the struggle against racism, and to teach one another.

People of color are frequently expected to speak on behalf of everyone of their race or ethnicity, or to represent the experiences of *every other* black or brown person—when, in truth, they can only speak from their own experiences. It is exhausting and emotionally draining to do this work; people of color have other full-time jobs they need to attend to, without having the added responsibility of always being the educators of white people. In many settings, people of color become the "token" diversity members, sitting on extra committees to ensure adequate representation of minority groups within an organization. This too, comes at an emotional cost. While representation is important, it is unfair to expect a small number of people to do extra work so white people can feel like we have taken into consideration their diverse perspectives. We need to do our *own* work, not only in educating ourselves, but also in educating other white people.

Faith communities are ideal places for these kinds of conversations. Persons know one another and tend to trust each other. In this atmosphere, we can accompany one another in our discomfort. Communities of faith are often still the most segregated groups within our society: you are more likely to be surrounded by persons of the same race when you are worshiping than when you are in school or at work. So if you are in a predominantly white congregation, it is especially important that white people take responsibility for educating one another, since there are few people of color in your midst to share their experiences, and those who are present are probably not eager to be the "token race person." We need to do our own work, and we need to do it in our faith communities.

3. What kind of accountability do you have to communities of color?

I have been asked this question before, and it comes from a place of appropriate suspicion. The suspicion is this: there is a long history of whites "speaking for" other groups, without fairly or honestly representing their views. How can you, the reader, trust that I am not going to perpetuate racism by unfairly representing the real struggle people of color continue to face?

For asking these questions, I say, "Thank you." Thank you for knowing about the challenges and pitfalls of whites talking about racism without actually committing to doing the work to dismantle racism and white privilege. Thank you for holding me accountable.

I also am continuing to grow and learn. I am part of a group of scholars who mostly come from Historically Black Colleges and Universities (HBCUs) in Texas. We are working on an Oral History Project to record personal stories of racial discrimination. I read the work of scholars of color who write and research racism and who write about the experiences of people of color in the U.S. Other scholars of religion and homiletics who are people of color have read my first book, heard me present at conferences, and support my work.

However, none of this makes me immune to racism or to perpetuating harmful stereotypes, or making mistakes that hurt others. So I ask for your prayers as I continue this work, that I will remain open to the discovery of new ideas, and remain grateful for the moments of repentance and conversion that I continue to have along the way.

I encourage the same of you, dear reader. If you are white, continue to develop relationships with persons of color and seek out their advice and counsel. A pastor friend of mine said that she realized talking about racism meant she needed to be in more places where she felt uncomfortable, being the minority in spaces where people of color were the majority. She expressed the feeling that she couldn't share stories with her congregation if she was not present with others who are experiencing these stories. If we are isolated, we cannot offer ways of bridging the divide within our own communities.

At the same time, do not turn to people of color to help you feel like a "good white person." We have to keep doing this work even when no one is there to tell us: "You're doing this right." As a character in Chimamanda Adichie's novel *Americanah* has said: "Racism should never have happened and so you don't get a cookie for reducing it." So please do not turn to people of color as a way of validating your work. At the same time, allow for people of color in your life to call you into a deeper engagement with the subject. Accountability is another way of saying: we are all in this together, and we need one another in order to make a difference.

4. How can I avoid sounding political?

Religious professionals have told me that their congregations are tired of the political divisiveness they see throughout the country, and their congregants do not want them to bring up "politics" in their preaching. Talking about racism in sermons sounds like taking a political stance. They wonder, "How can I focus on preaching about racism when members may *leave* if they think I'm 'too political'?"

Politics are never value-neutral nor faith-neutral. Persons making political decisions base those decisions on their own values as well as on their beliefs about faith. People who share the same faith tradition can vote very differently from one another and support different policies based on what they value. Key for religious leaders who live in "purple areas," where there are numbers of people on both sides of the political spectrum, is to focus on values shared in common. Rather than telling persons to vote a certain way on candidates or policies, encourage conversations about who is impacted by the decisions of political candidates and their policies. Listen to perspectives that share different values.

At the same time, scriptures from all the world's religious traditions are clear about caring for those who are suffering, those who are oppressed, those who have been treated unjustly. When having these conversations in your congregation, are persons who have been treated unjustly represented? Do they have voice in these conversations? The goal is not to try to make members vote a certain way, but rather to build bridges toward greater understanding.

Racism is always political. It impacts the "*polis*," or the "body of citizens," of a society. Political decisions to legalize slavery and segregation had to be overturned and outlawed by other political measures. A presidential order from Franklin D. Roosevelt forced Japanese American citizens to relocate to internment camps during World War II, and later presidential action by Presidents Carter and Reagan tried to make amends to the survivors and their heirs. It took political moves to grant citizenship to African Americans, women, and immigrants who were deemed "not white." The Civil Rights legislation of the 1960s addressed ongoing practices of discrimination, but there are still ways people are treated unjustly today. Invite your congregation into deeper conversations, not about political parties or candidates, but about the history of how political decisions have impacted communities in your area. Who has been negatively impacted? What role has race played in these outcomes?

It is not easy to discuss racism in congregations. Calling it "political" is true, but it is also a way of saying, "I'm uncomfortable talking about this." Invite members of your congregation who feel this way into conversation, listen to their stories, and, with compassion, invite them to stay engaged amidst their discomfort.

5. Are you crazy? I could lose my job!

This is a real fear, and I do not want to minimize the risks you take. As a minister, you are often facing immense pressure to meet the expectations of your congregants. When ministers fail to meet those expectations, either through inadequately fulfilling the duties of a pastor or upsetting the members, they have been let go or sent to other (and perhaps less desirable) church positions, depending on the polity of the denomination. Taking on a controversial subject you know may make listeners upset with you can be a very daunting task.

That is why I want to help you do this. I want to support you in this difficult work and to give you strategies for preaching about racism in your congregation. I want to encourage you, to help you muster your bravery, and to suggest that there may be more people in your congregation who are wanting you to address this subject than you may yet realize. You may be surprised. I have encountered persons who have grown up in the Deep South, who I would have never guessed would be receptive to talking about racism, come up to me with tears in their eyes, grateful I spoke about it.

I know this is hard. And yet having responded to the call to ministry, you have already been doing hard things for a long time. I'm grateful to you for continuing the conversation. My prayers go with you on this journey.

Chapter 1

Preaching to Ourselves: Beginning with Gratitude

In light of your busy schedule, dear preacher, let me cut to the chase: preaching about racism needs to come from a place of gratitude.

Not shame, not guilt, but gratitude.

Gratitude is what motivates us to preach about racism: we do this work to share with persons we love the ways they can know more fully the breadth of community God is calling us to experience, and to point to the work of God already in our midst, redeeming the brokenness of the world.

Gratitude as our motivation means we engage in these conversations in the same way that we tell people about the best aspects of our faith. Sharing this good news comes from a place of gratitude: God has redeemed us, and we are still being redeemed. And we want to tell the world about this good news.

It seems counterintuitive to speak of gratitude and good news when you're talking about something as terrible as racism. And gratitude is complex: in the history of race in this country, whites told enslaved Africans to "be grateful" for the kindness of their slaveholders. More recently, persons of color have been insulted with the words such as: "You should be grateful we even let you into this country!" Demands for gratitude or expectations for others to be grateful are oppressive. Demanding gratitude is not "good news."

Instead, I place no demands on you to "be grateful," and I encourage you *not* to tell your congregation to be grateful, but I will also *invite you* to see how gratitude can help people envision talking about racism in new ways.

As a Christian preacher, I have been called to proclaim the good news of Jesus Christ. But as a *white* preacher, I have a special calling—to name the sin of racism that has plagued white Christians for hundreds of years, to help other preachers do the same, and to help white people find ways of living that acknowledges their whiteness, and yet no longer allows subconscious assumptions of white superiority to go unchallenged in themselves or in others.

For the past 10 years, I've been mulling over this question: How can white preachers preach about racism to predominantly white congregations? The question followed me as I graduated from seminary and entered ministry, serving first as a hospital chaplain on the U.S.-Mexico border, and then as an associate pastor in a majority-white congregation in Texas. The question kept demanding my attention as I became associate director of admissions for Princeton Seminary. The question became so persistent that I enrolled in an additional master's degree program, studying part-time while continuing to work full-time as a seminary administrator. I focused on the history of African American preaching traditions and white preachers' attempts to address racism in the past, as well as black theologians' responses to racism. I felt like I was just scratching the surface. By then, the question was so loud I could not deny that I was being called to find an answer: How can I help other white pastors like me talk about racism? So in 2010 I left a good job with benefits to pursue a Ph.D., just after the major economic recession, when voluntarily giving up a good job to enter academia (where the jobs are already scarce) was considered *crazy*. But the question kept calling, and I had to answer.

As I moved into my Ph.D. studies at Emory University, I began finding more interdisciplinary approaches to understanding racism, drawing from linguistic anthropology, philosophies of justice, theologies of sin, and narrative theories. Consistent themes that emerged include how the word *racism* has changed over time, and that racism is hard to understand if you are not a person of color. These two themes developed for me into the challenge of recognizing racism and the challenge for whites of recognizing ourselves as white within a racist society.

As I approached the dissertation-writing stage of my program, I discovered a book by Paul Ricoeur, a hermeneutic philosopher whom I had studied during a seminar taught by my Ph.D. advisor, Tom Long. Ricoeur's book *The Course of Recognition,* a published series of lectures delivered shortly before he died, centers on the challenges of *recognition* in three senses: cognition, identity, and gratitude.[1] These three forms of recognition gave me a framework for describing the challenges I saw white people encountering when talking about racism.

Focusing on recognition as having a *cognitive* component put a label on the challenge of different definitions and understandings of the word *racism.* At the same time, simply understanding the word *racism* did not clear things up. Definitions of racism may not translate to a deeper recognition of racism's ongoing presence in the world. In my experience, it often took listening to how racism impacts real people to recognize it: hearing and seeing that, yes, racism is real, and much more prevalent than we previously thought.

The *identity* aspect for whites, recognizing ourselves as *white*, and needing to change personally and as part of a larger unjust system, also proved challenging, creating discomfort and a sense of identity-disorientation. If we are to recognize ourselves within the history and legacy of racism, we have to talk about how racism has impacted *all* people in society, and confront the distortion of our identity resulting from the racial violence that has given priority to whites and dehumanized persons of color.

For those of us who are white, the recognition of our white identity creates significant challenges for talking about racism. This is where racial identity development theory[2] can be a tremendous help. The theory, developed by psychologists, clarifies the predictable *emotions* that emerge when learning about racism. The stages of developing a racial identity point a way toward a healthier self-understanding for whites, even while learning how to challenge racism in society.

Ricoeur's third element of recognition includes a turn toward *gratitude*, since recognition's definition includes this "unexpected guest" of a meaning. Gratitude is often expressed as recognition—"I want to recognize everyone who helped me get to where I am today." Recognition points us outward in gratitude toward others. This final element of the framework became a radical discovery: What if, instead of preaching toward guilt, our preaching on racism could move us to *gratitude*?

But what could gratitude have to do with talking about racism?

Here is where the light bulbs started going off for me. I felt the connection between gratitude and the good news I'm called to preach. The text known as the "great commission," to "go...and make disciples" (Mt. 28:19), which is in many ways the first Christian call to go and preach, takes place after Jesus' resurrection. We preach because of the good news of Jesus Christ, the news that God did not let sin and death have the final say, but instead raised Jesus from the dead, declaring victory over sin and death. If you are a religious leader from a different faith tradition, what is the "good news" that you share with your members? And how does gratitude play a role in the communication of that good news?

For me, awareness of sin and God's response to sin had been a central part of my religious formation as a young person, attending youth group and the Fellowship of Christian Athletes and other high school campus ministries. From scripture, I learned that humans are sinners—that we have all sinned and fallen short of God's glory (Rom. 3:23)—and yet Christ died for us. Christ rose for us. And Christ reigns for us. That is *good news*; I don't go out and try to live differently because I feel guilty for what Christ has done. The shame of sin does not motivate us to live new lives. We let our love for God drive us. Our gratitude for what God has done gets us excited to live humbly and to work for justice. Gratitude is what motivates us.

Within liberal Christianity, preachers have tended to avoid *sin* language because of the ways it has been used harmfully in the past.[3] At the same time, deeper reflection on our theological language can be a helpful way of communicating the large-scale societal and spiritual effects of racism. The idea of "original sin," that all people are born into sin before they have committed actual "sins," may not be a popular theological concept in mainline Christianity; however, after learning about the history and legacy of racism, the concept of sin as being inherited makes more sense to me. Even Calvinism's seemingly draconian notion of "total depravity" (the idea that sin infects all of us and all of society) helps me articulate how racism can keep showing up in even the most well-meaning people and places. And the sense of shame and guilt that I once felt when talking about sin resonates with how I feel when confronting the reality of my complicity in racism.

Language about sin can help us describe with greater accuracy the widespread harm that racism inflicts upon *all* people. It also points to the source of our hope, in that our faith declares God's redemption of sin. Because sin language leads us to talking about redemption, it does not leave us in despair. Talking about sin points us to God, toward our hoped-for-futures, and the *telos* of how God created us to live in community with one another.

Not Recovered, but in Recovery

For many white people, there is a lot of discomfort in talking about racism. Some of that discomfort stems from the fact that we cannot change the color of our skin. We can't just repent of racism and say we are no longer "white," because society still sees us as white. Even if we name our "white privilege," that privilege still continues to follow us whether we want it to or not.[4] Examples of this include the kind of treatment white kids receive from their teachers in school.[5] If we go to get a mortgage, we are more likely to be approved and get the best interest rates.[6] If we want to live in a "nice" neighborhood, we don't have to worry about someone telling us the house we want to buy is suddenly "off the market," and wondering if it was because of the color of our skin.[7] We will not be asked to show proof of our citizenship, forced to carry around our papers wherever we go lest we get thrown into a deportation holding center.[8] When we get upset, we don't have to worry about someone calling us an "angry black man or woman."[9] When we get pulled over for speeding, we don't have to worry whether we will make it home alive.[10]

We can't change the color of our skin. If you're white, you cannot *stop* being *white*. But as sinners, we never stop being *sinners*, either. We never get to the point where we can say: I am sinless. As persons who have gone through recovery programs for alcohol or drug addiction may say: "We are *in recovery*, not *recovered*." As persons of faith, we never reach perfection. As white people, we need to remember that we can never get to the point of being totally anti-racist or free of racism. This is important because too often we assume we are innocent and that we are not racist; we assume we are not to blame for the problems of racism. But as persons living in a society still divided by race, benefitting unfairly from these social divisions, we need to acknowledge that we will continue to be part of the problem even when we try our best to work against racism.

However, here is where our gratitude comes in. This is also where the language of faith helps me articulate the personal impact of learning about racism and how it impacts our relationship with God. Confession leads to gratitude, when we recognize God's continual work and presence in our lives.

Gratitude emerges when we realize that, while we still fall short of our religious ideals, while we who are white still benefit from unfair advantages, God is still working in us and through us. God continues to use us to do good work, even if imperfectly. We give thanks for the lives of men and women who have gone before us, who have shown us how to courageously stand up for what is right—even while they themselves were far from perfect. Gratitude that God is still working in us and through us gives us the courage we need and the humility to go out and try again and again at our feeble attempts to make this world a better place.

Gratitude also flows from us when we recognize the gifts this journey brings us. When others share their painful stories with us, when someone tells us a story of how they have experienced discrimination, we feel deep gratitude, knowing that sharing such stories can often feel like reopening a wound. We look at the history of segregation, and we are grateful that community and communion is happening across racial lines even in spite of this dreadful past. For the loved ones in our lives who call us to greater awareness of racial discrimination, we give thanks.

Gratitude is also a process, an invitation to stay engaged. When strong emotions of others make us feel threatened or defensive, we may not automatically feel grateful. But we can remind ourselves that sharing in a difficult conversation is a gift, and, instead of responding defensively, we can ask ourselves, "How can I respond with gratitude? What am I thankful for in this interaction? How is what this person is sharing a gift to me?" We can create new habits in ourselves of cultivating gratitude, even in the midst of painful and challenging conversations.[11] This happens across racial lines, as well as when we are talking with other white people who do not share our same perspective. Staying engaged in difficult relationships can result from our commitment to gratitude.

Gratitude also involves our own participation—recognizing that we have gifts to share with others. We feel grateful that God has given each of us individual gifts, placing us in particular spheres of influence where we can have these conversations with others. We are grateful because we have been called to work and to participate in God's continuing kin-dom building.[12] We express gratitude for being called to live differently, to live into the new life God has for us, and to celebrate the relationships and community God is preparing for us.

For all this, we say, "Thank you!" Gratitude starts with you, faith leader, accepting that you have gifts to offer the world in addressing this challenging subject. I am thankful for you, and I hope you hear this message as a sermon to yourself (as I hear it speaking to me) that you have gifts to share; so thank you.

Strategies for Preaching: Start with Gratitude

1. Find your own place of gratitude: What are the gifts you have received along the way that have prompted you to preach about racism?

2. What are the gifts you are being called to share with others?

3. What are the gifts of your congregation that they bring to these conversations?

Chapter 2

The Role of Interpretation and Recognition

Interpretation is what you do all day in your job. As a preacher, you are making meaning of the sacred text of your tradition and the congregation's situation, interpreting how to make sense of recent tragic events on the news, and trying to discern what the people need to hear from God. This is a heavy responsibility.

In preparing to preach, the job of making meaning by interpreting the world and the sacred text is complex. For example, I sit down to read an ancient text such as the first chapter in Genesis, and my mind begins making connections: linking the words on the page to a story about creation, recalling how this passage has been used to debate evolution, considering what this text means for our care of the environment, and reflecting on what it means for humankind to be made "in the image of God" (1:27). Add to that the struggles of the congregation: What does this text mean for communities who have been hit by a hurricane or other natural disaster, who wonder whether God really is in control of the world? Or persons feeling worthless because of abusive relationships, or unemployment, or debilitating illness, doubting they resemble the image of God in any way? The job of preaching requires interpreting the text at the same time as you are interpreting the lived situation of your congregation and the world in which we live.

Layers of meaning compete for your attention. Which ones will you give voice to in the sermon? Where, in all of this, is a message from God?

I am a preacher, but that is not my only identity. I am also a mother, a wife, a professor, a daughter, a scholar. I am a woman. I am also white. All of these different parts of my identity impact my interpretation of the text. As a mother, I look at the Genesis 1 text and wonder, "How can I help my science-loving son see that the biblical account of creation does not have to be at odds with science?" As a woman, I think, "I really prefer this first creation account (man and woman created in God's image) to the one that comes just after it (God forming Adam from the dust, then Eve from

15

Adam's rib), because the first emphasizes the equality of men and women as equally made in God's image, and the second has been used harmfully to portray women as subordinate." As a professor of preaching, I wonder: "What is the main claim this text is making, and how does that form the focus of the sermon?"

But where does my whiteness come into this? Typically, it doesn't. I have no reason from my own experience as a white person to connect this story of creation with my racial identity. Not having experienced racism as my daily reality, it is not something in the forefront of my mind. The notion of race appears in my mind as an afterthought, an add-on, an extra—only relevant if there is something in the news that calls my attention to racism. I may not imagine racism as regularly impacting the people of my congregation. "My people," I may think, "have other, more pressing issues they are dealing with and that I need to attend to." If you are a leader of a Jewish or Muslim faith community, maybe you all have been targeted by anti-Semitism or anti-Muslim sentiments. If your community of faith is composed of people who are oppressed because of their sexual orientation, your congregation is familiar with heterosexism, and you may not feel the need to address other "-isms." Why focus on racism when your community is already facing its own forms of oppression?

Imagining ourselves in someone else's shoes may help. What if we imagined ourselves as having been racialized differently by society? What if our skin color made us stand out among our peers as being different, or if we only saw negative stereotypes in the media of people who looked like ourselves? What if in these and many other small and relentless ways we were constantly being told, "You are *not like us*. You are *less beautiful*. You are *not the norm. We are not the same*." Or, if, as we were driving in our cars, we were fearful that we might die or be deported if pulled over by the police? If that were our daily experience, then how might we read this first chapter of Genesis differently?

God created *all* of humankind in God's image: white folks, black folks, brown folks, persons from every country across the world. *All* folks. All of humankind in the image of God—with various shapes to our eyes and noses, beautiful varieties of hair colors and textures, skin all the colors of God's good earth. "God saw everything that [God] had made, and indeed, it was very good" (1:31). We are *all* part of God's creation. We are no different from one another, just variations on a theme.

Now, this may lead me to preach a very different sermon than one that focused on the environment or on the relationship between science and the Bible. Or, maybe, all of these meanings would somehow make their way into the sermon. The creative process that leads to the final sermon is varied and complicated, dependent on our individual personalities and the ways we tend to work.

However, before that process begins, there is interpretation. Before the sermon comes together in any kind of shape, there is the making of meaning: bringing together the text with the concerns of the people and the world in which we live. But *which* concerns will you bring with you to the text? *Whose world* are you living in as you consider what issues most impact your reading? And if our default is to read the text through our own eyes, with the limitations of our own interpretive horizons, how can we address the greater diversity of concerns that our listeners bring with them on Sunday morning? How can we broaden our own interpretive frameworks?

We are regularly tempted to use our default interpretive lenses, viewing the text for how it most directly relates to our own experience and the experience of persons we know. That is our quickest go-to tool. It is easiest for us to imagine how the text relates to us individually, and then also to people we can imagine and empathize with.

I could respond by trying to guilt you or shame you into considering others' points of view, but I don't think that is a helpful approach. I could tell you about Jesus loving everyone, having compassion for persons very different from him, always widening his circle of concern, but you know this already. I could point out the commandments present in other sacred texts that speak to our responsibility for the well-being of others. Instead, let me turn to testimony, sharing my own experience of sensing what was wrong with my standard frame of interpreting the Bible. I share this testimony to point to the unconscious role of interpretation, but also to remind you of the centrality of testimony in this work: helping others see how we ourselves have changed is an invitation to allow others into our view of the world without judgment. We can be the first to say: I have not always viewed the world this way, and here's how I changed.

Removing My Blinders

I grew up as a cradle Presbyterian and the great-granddaughter of a Methodist minister, attending church two or three times a week. I knew all the answers in Sunday school, asked difficult theological questions of my teachers, attended the Fellowship of Christian Athletes beginning in middle school, and became a student leader in our high school campus ministry. Called to ministry at the age of 15, I wanted to prepare for a life of Christian service. I majored in religion in college, focusing on Christian spirituality, worked as a youth intern with the middle schoolers at the local church, and volunteered as a chaplain to sick children at a hospital. I was reading the Bible daily and spending quiet time with God in prayer. While far from perfect, I was trying to live as faithfully as I could.

After college, I went to seminary to qualify for ordination in my denomination. It was there in seminary, at the age of 21, that I first realized racism was not a thing of the past, and not a thing only perpetuated by KKK members, but something that is ongoing, persistent, and experienced in hundreds of little ways every day by people of color. What shocked me about this realization was that I never heard anything about ongoing racism while growing up in predominantly white Christian contexts. I thought the civil rights movement had achieved its goals, and those achievements were set in stone. I hadn't heard the stories of people of color who get pulled over by police for broken taillights or driving in a "white" neighborhood—where they live—and having these kinds of experiences on a regular basis. Hearing these stories brought racism to life for me in new ways.

One especially poignant moment of my conversion came about with something as mundane as a course syllabus. At the end of my first year in seminary, I had started to consider how being a woman may have impacted me in my faith; I realized I wasn't the only one who had experienced doubts about my calling, because men and women in my life had told me, "God doesn't call women to be pastors." I was reading other women theologians who were sharing their stories of how God called them nevertheless, empowering them to use their voices to proclaim God's good news and to help other women find their voices. So I wanted to take a course on this subject.

But the only one offered in the fall was on Feminist and Womanist Theologies. I took a look at the syllabus, and each week was looking at theology from a different perspective—there were Asian women theologians, Hispanic women theologians, African women theologians, African American women theologians, Asian American women theologians, and so forth. I was looking at the syllabus with my boyfriend at the time, and I said something like, "You know, I'm not sure I want to take this. I really just want plain feminist theology." Inside, I was thinking to myself, "I will not be able to relate to these other women's experiences. Their contexts are so different from my own that it won't be helpful to me."

Here's what happened. My boyfriend, the man who would later become my husband, said this: "You know, I think that's where feminist theology is going these days—seeing how women from all over the world can help us understand more about God, and that feminism isn't just about white women's experiences, but every woman's experiences."

Boom. It was a gentle comment, said without judgment, but I felt like a mirror had just been brought to my face for the first time. I was not just a generic woman. I was a *white* woman—and me not expecting to be able to learn something from these other women was like men assuming they had nothing to learn from me because I was a woman.

I, unfortunately, was a racist. Without intending to be, without harboring hate toward people of color, never considering myself to have a racist bone in my body, I was part of a racist system, and that meant *I was less likely to see women of color as being able to tell me about who God is.*

That moment became a watershed for me. I began noticing more and more the times when I would recognize racism in myself. I stopped in Trenton, New Jersey, as I was driving through, and I pulled over to get gas in a predominantly black neighborhood. I realized that seeing myself surrounded by people of color made me fearful. I noticed this fear, and so I asked myself: *What are you afraid of? That you will get mugged? How likely is it that you will have money stolen from you here, when people on Wall Street are stealing money in much larger amounts? Why would I assume people of color would steal from me, when white people are also thieves? Think of all the land white people stole from Native Americans, or the labor we stole from enslaved Africans.*

These moments of recognition were painful. I didn't want to think of myself as a racist. I was raised to think of racism as something only really bad people did and said. And here I was, embodying the same kind of racism that I assumed was only spoken aloud by using hateful racial slurs or burning crosses. But racism can be much more subtle, which makes it even more insidious.

Sometimes it's unconscious—people have unconscious biases that they act on instantaneously. Biologically, our bodies respond to our own prejudices and biases; when we assume someone we meet is dangerous, our stress levels are going to increase and we will not make good decisions. This is why so many people are calling for greater education and training for police officers across the country. The police have a very dangerous job. And they are also armed with deadly weapons. If they are afraid of a person, they are more likely to reach for their gun. If society has taught these officers to be afraid of black men, then it will be black men who will get guns pulled on them, even though white men regularly perpetuate mass shootings in our country.

But if we haven't been taught to see this, if our eyes are not accustomed to noticing the bias at work in ourselves or in our society at large, then we will go around with blinders on, only paying attention to what impacts us most directly. And what we pay attention to directly affects how we read scripture, how we interpret the Bible or our other sacred texts, and how we prepare sermons to preach in our congregations.

One of my beliefs when it comes to talking about racism is that guilt and shame are not adequate long-term motivators or sustainers for this difficult work. So I do not want to point out our blinders and suggest that you should feel guilty for having them. There are a lot of ways we have blinders to the pain of others! That is why it is so important for us to keep learning from one another. What I find more sustaining in this work is the deep gratitude I feel for the grace of God working in me on this issue, seeing my mistakes along the way and still encouraging me to go out and say something. I believe gratitude can help us stay engaged in this work.

The Challenges of Recognition

In preaching about racism in your context, the difficulty lies not just in overcoming your own interpretative blinders and becoming able to recognize racism, but also in the challenges many of your listeners may have in interpreting and recognizing racism. Based on the three forms of "recognition" discussed in the previous chapter, it is helpful to consider how your congregants may struggle with recognizing racism: coming to cognitive awareness of what racism means, recognizing the significance of being identified as a particular "race" in a racialized society, and moving out of emotional resistance and toward active anti-racism.

First, a challenge in preaching about racism is that, at least for many white people, we have a hard time recognizing what racism means on an experiential level. We may be able to look at the 2017 "Unite the Right" rally in Charlottesville, with white guys holding torches, yelling Nazi chants, and say, "Yes—*that's* racism!" When the news cycle turns to some other event, we may quickly move on to other concerns, without feeling the real existential threat that hate groups present to us or our families. It may be easy for us to recognize some instances of racism, but not others. We may see racism in individual acts of intentional harm and racial hatred, but racism is not just about individual acts. White people have a hard time seeing racism as a larger whole, a system that is bigger than individual comments and "personal preferences" put together.

And yet giving people definitions does not necessarily help them to see racism differently. I was on the radio discussing my first book with radio host Jennifer Stayton of KUT, Austin's NPR station. Stayton asked me how I defined racism, and I answered:

> Racism is a system that creates unfair advantages for whites, while disproportionately penalizing persons of color. This isn't a new concept; it's something that was forged in the beginnings of the trans-Atlantic slave trade, justifying why we should be able to have people as property. And this racism, this warped imagination, is what continues to keep some people in disadvantaged positions compared to whites. So my definition of racism has a particular context in that it is something that I view as a system; it's not something that's just individual hate acts of one person saying a bad word or an offensive phrase, but it's this larger system that has infected us. That's part of the air we breathe. That's something that we need to be able to uncover so that we can work toward eradicating it.[1]

Now this was a question I answered on the spot, without notes, on the radio. Others have written about the meaning of racism with much greater insight.[2] But basically, I wanted to communicate that racism is broader than individual acts and that racism benefits white people.

However, upon hearing that definition, a listener responded by emailing me to critique my definition, citing the experience of having grown up white in a town where the majority were Latinx. Focusing on the definition for racism I provided, he felt I was discounting his experience as a white "minority," and resisted further engagement. The author of this email confirms that defining "racism" only helps so much. For some people, it can be illuminating. For others, it becomes a stumbling block, a way to put the brakes on the conversation.

I also grew up in a town with a large population of Latinx.[3] But not being aware of the realities of racism, I did not understand how racism and colorism impacted the Latinx community or my place as a white person in a position of privilege. Persons who identify as Latinx can be "white" as well as "black," because of the complicated history of colonization, conquest of indigenous people, and slavery throughout Spanish-speaking countries and Latin America. In Puerto Rico, where some of the population is black and others are white, there is a "colorism" in which lighter-skinned Puerto Ricans are treated better than darker-skinned Puerto Ricans. A woman I interviewed for an oral history project shared how her father was a dark-skinned Puerto Rican, like his father. She was much lighter-skinned, like her mother. At her grandfather's deathbed, he looked at her skin and told her she was "improving the race," a "compliment" that made her feel ashamed and confused.

So yes, racism is not just present within white communities. And examples from around the world confirm that people can be racist against persons they decide are racially different, such as when white Jews were killed by white Germans in the Holocaust. And yet, while there are examples of racism impacting "whites," there is a tendency around the world to give preference to those who are lighter-skinned, and this preference confers unearned advantages to those who are lighter-skinned.

The point of definitions is to gain clarity on a subject; however, racism as a "subject" constantly defies clarification. Racism has to do with our experiences of the world, encounters with other people, and subtle as well as overt messages communicated through body language, speech, and visual representations. Scholar Helen Ngo describes racism as the experience of not-being-at-home in one's body.[4] Such an experience defies explanation in a logical, linear way that others can cognitively grasp. Because it is hard for many whites to "recognize racism," it is important that preachers try to communicate the experiences of racism in narrative form that can help listeners better understand.

The second challenge in preaching about racism, particularly in white contexts, is that white people have a hard time recognizing the significance of their white identity, and it is easier for whites to avoid thinking about their own race. For white people, recognizing ourselves as white tends to mark us as the bad guys. It makes us feel uncomfortable. Many of us were taught to not talk about race growing up—it was impolite. We were taught to be "colorblind." We may have never considered how being colorblind may have hidden our own biases from ourselves. To name race already feels like we are doing something transgressive, as if naming race is itself racist. If we do not believe ourselves to be racist, then we may resist naming ourselves as white, since it feels as if we are identifying with white supremacists. These perceptions make us want to avoid the conversation altogether.

The listener who responded to the definition of racism I used in my radio interview exemplifies the challenge of identifying ourselves as white. He felt that connecting the word *racism* to the concept of "systemic racism" was too far of a mental jump, since it is easier for listeners to see individual acts of discrimination as the true problem of racism. But the reason this is a mental jump for many is because it links "good" white people—persons who do not act intentionally to discriminate—to the larger problems of racism as seen in this broader system. When we view ourselves as "*good* white people," and now we are being indicted in a larger set of problems, our own self-identity goes into disorientation. We resist responsibility for the larger problems of racial inequality because we do not see ourselves as causing those problems out of malicious intent.

It is crucial that preachers connect white listeners to these larger systems, helping them to see how they benefit from the racial inequality that they themselves do not cause, and how responding to this inequality requires us to have compassion on ourselves. Our emotional responses to talking about racism can derail our conversations if we are not attentive to how our self-perceptions are put into turmoil when we identify as white beneficiaries of a racist society. We cannot make white people feel bad about themselves in order to encourage them to be part of the solution, but neither can we let white people view themselves as "the *good* white people" who are exempt from needing to have these conversations. All of us need to be part of the solution, but our participation often depends on our first being able to identify ourselves as part of the problem. Recognizing ourselves as white, and having compassion for ourselves during the emotional and psychological ups-and-downs that accompany that recognition, is an important part of the process.

The third challenge in preaching about racism is helping listeners move beyond their emotional resistance and toward active anti-racism, which I believe occurs through the practice of gratitude. In learning about racism, we often don't know what we can do about it; we cannot recognize a proper response. We are afraid of saying the wrong thing or sounding racist, and we are at a loss as to what we can actually do to change things. It is hard for us to respond in gratitude for these challenging conversations; we may be more likely to respond with defensiveness, anger, guilt, or an anxious desire to do something quickly.

At the end of different diversity trainings I've been in or conversations about racism I have led, there is often this request at the end: "What can we do? Tell us what to do." This is a good impulse; we want to change the world and make it more just for everyone. It is good to want to do something different, to change society, and to address this wrong that has been going on for so long.

But at the same time, the impulse to do something can be a way of moving too quickly to a solution, of trying to fix a problem that we cannot solve on our own. When we strongly want to *do* something, it can sometimes come out of a place of wanting to feel better—to address our discomfort. Talking about racism makes us feel uncomfortable, and we don't like to feel this way. Our subconscious may urge us to find a solution so we can go back to feeling better. This may mean that our impulse to do something about racism then becomes, first and foremost, about *us*.

This is not to say that we do not need to act; responding to racism does indeed require us to act in real and tangible ways. At the same time, active anti-racism requires a longer committment than our initial impulses to resolve our negative feelings by doing something just to make *us* feel better. I want us to help our congregations recognize this impulse and help us sit with our discomfort, accepting that we cannot solve this problem on our own. We need to be able to build relationships with communities who are already working against racism in our area, turning to the leadership of others who have been doing this work longer than we have. And yet again, particularly for white people, we need to be slow to turn to people of color as a way of absolving us of our guilt, avoiding the impulse to put responsibility for our education about racism back onto people of color rather than taking responsibility for our own learning.

I also recognize that we all have limits to what we can do; our families need us, people have jobs and other things to do. Members of our congregations may not feel free to go out and become full-time activists against racism. It can be challenging to feel a response is possible when all of us already lead such busy lives and the problem is so big.

One way we can encourage one another is to invite each other to be fully present in the conversation, to make a commitment within the community to listen to the hard stories and experiences of others, and to learn more about how racism continues to operate in our society. We all have gifts that we can use; we just have to learn what those gifts are in relationship to working against racism. Each one of us has our own circle of influence. Helping our congregations identify where they are gifted can connect them back to that sense of gratitude, helping us acknowledge that

God has gifted all of humanity in unique ways, and to look for how we can put those gifts into God's service.

As leaders of faith communities, you are on the front lines. There is a lot going on in our society and in our churches and organizations, so it is easy to assume this is yet another "issue" competing for our attention. But our integrity as spiritual leaders is on the line. We are being called to open up our story to the God who interrupts the status quo, and to seek out how our story may be changing. Being on the front lines gives you an opportunity to lead in your communities, and to invite those you serve into re-imagining their stories as well, increasing their capacity to hear the stories of the suffering of others and inviting them to make a difference where they can.

Seeing the challenges of recognizing racism, recognizing ourselves as racialized, and recognizing how to best respond through gratitude, we can identify preaching strategies to help our congregants through these forms of recognition, and overcome our own anxiety about addressing racism from the pulpit. The deeper motivation for us, and what we hope to convey to those in our care, is the sense of gratitude for what God is doing in these hard conversations, and gratitude for the chance to offer our own gifts to the struggle.

These three categories structure my approach to preaching about racism: helping listeners recognize what we mean by the word *racism,* helping listeners to see themselves as racialized and to accept their complicated feelings about their "race," and, finally, moving toward gratitude as a response to learning about racism. If our sermons and teaching can recognize our listeners' own challenges and journey along with them, then together we can grow and learn more fully how being anti-racist is an integral part of our faith journey.

Strategies for Preaching: Three Forms of Recognition

1. Consider how your listeners may come from different perspectives when it comes to defining the word *racism.* Consider using stories in your sermons to help broaden the understanding of your congregation.

2. Imagine what challenges your listeners have seeing themselves as racialized in society. Help hearers identify with the persons typically seen as the "other" in the scripture text, and how that may help give insight into our current social context.

3. Picture gratitude as a rooting metaphor and motivation for your preaching about racism. Help listeners find hope in the redeeming work of Jesus Christ, evoking gratitude for what God is already doing in our midst.

Chapter 3

Communicating What Racism Means

To preach about racism and to interpret sacred texts in light of the continuing harm of racism, we need to be clear in our minds about what we mean by the word *racism*. In our preaching and teaching, we may have something very specific in our minds, but this meaning may vary significantly from what is in the minds of our listeners. Naming the difficulty of recognizing racism means that we understand the challenges of communicating an idea that has changed over time. The words associated with racism may differ depending on what part of the world you live in, or what region of the United States your church community calls home. Connotations with the word *racism* may even differ by neighborhood.

In some neighborhoods, racism refers to the over-policing of the poor, making it more likely that poor persons of color will be arrested and put in prison. In other neighborhoods, racism may refer to the assumption—expressed verbally or indirectly—that "you do not belong here" if you are black or brown and living in a predominantly white area. Racism may include assumptions that Native Americans have died out, or the colorism in Latinx communities that privileges lighter-skinned persons over those with darker skin. It may also mean the constant question posed to Asian Americans that casts them as perpetual foreigners: "Where are you *really* from?" It could refer to parties where whites wear costumes such as sombreros, headdresses, or blackface that mock other groups and perpetuate a long history of stereotyped misrepresentation of other groups. The word *racism* may also conjure up the different treatment immigrants of color have received compared to immigrants from white countries: the political rhetoric around "building a wall" between the U.S. and Mexico is very different than how politicians speak about the Canadian border, for instance.

In other areas, however, racism may conjure up the image of a white person getting passed over for a job or admission to college in favor of "affirmative action" hires or acceptances. The word *racism* may be associated with "race baiting" or trying to stir up controversy for the sake of controversy, or playing the "race card" for personal benefit. Some listeners may think about the conversation of racism today is itself a form of racism against white people.

In the midst of very different perspectives on what we mean by the word *racism,* as a white preacher you face two potential pitfalls. The first is the assumption that listeners agree with your own analysis of what racism means, when, in their minds, they have something else in mind entirely. The second pitfall is an overreliance on jargon, or words that some may immediately understand while others are feeling left behind and resentful. Jargon includes words that are abstract and refer to a larger theory or body of knowledge. If you have attended a diversity training session or anti-racism workshop, you may have in your vocabulary a few of these words that may come off as jargon to your listeners. Words such as *systemic, privilege, power, supremacy*—even *racial identity development,* which I cover later in this book—can all come across as jargon. These words are very helpful tools in understanding racism as systemic, related to white privilege, connected to power dynamics, and summarized by assumptions of white supremacy. At the same time, handing your listeners a bunch of jargon they are unfamiliar with, or perhaps know but do not understand or agree with, may be alienating to your listeners. Explaining racism with new definitions may also communicate that being anti-racist simply requires learning a new language.

Back Story: Why Racism Means Different Things to Different People

In my studies, I have read several definitions of racism. Michael Emerson and Christian Smith define racism as, "...the collective misuse of power that harms another racial group, it is rational, and it includes the justifications provided for racialization."[1] Eduardo Bonilla-Silva has used the term "color-blind racism" to talk about the subtle ways race perpetuates itself in a society that prides itself on being colorblind toward racial difference.[2] A more concise definition of racism as "racial prejudice plus power" is frequently used in anti-racism workshops.[3]

The reason why definitions of racism differ, and why these definitions may not coincide with the "common sense" of most white Christians' understanding of racism, is that racism as an idea is constantly evolving. The work of Michael Omi and Howard Winant describes this as a social process of racial formation, in which the meaning of race and racism is constantly changing and politically contested, based on current race relations in a historical period.[4]

How we talk about race and racism has changed over time. For instance, many members of our congregations may have lived long enough to remember discussions about race before the desegregation of public schools. The discussion of racism then centered around whether or not you supported integration. Now, though "separate but equal" is illegal, schools and neighborhoods continue to be segregated, and the conversation about what racism means and how inequality perpetuates itself needs to be discussed. As we move through history, and current theories of racism fail to explain persistent problems, new challenges to a commonsense understanding of racism can emerge.

This is true of the concept of race as well; race as a categorical marker has itself shifted across history.[5] Race is not a biological designation, and yet there have been times in history when racial categorization was its own science. Race is a social construct, through which certain features of the human body or a person's country of origin or religious affiliation have been selected to classify a person within a racial group. The grouping together of persons into races is a way of categorizing people that has historically been used in the United States for the social domination of one group—white Protestant Christian citizens of the United States—over all others.

But who has counted as white also has shifted over time. For instance, Syrians in the early 20th century argued successfully in court to be allowed citizenship on the basis of being white, and since the 1960s Arabs and other persons from the Middle East have been listed as white on the U.S. Census. However, following September 11, 2001, this same group became the object of intense racial profiling.[6] This shift in treatment from being seen as white to becoming a target for racial profiling demonstrates race as a changing marker of identity, a concept that is not static but continues to change. Omi and Winant write: *"Race is a concept which signifies and symbolizes social conflicts and interests by referring to different types of human bodies...*[where] selection of these particular human features for purposes of racial stratification is always and necessarily a social and historical process."[7] Other conflicts through which "race" has been transformed include the Supreme Court cases of Ozawa and Thind, in which the plaintiffs argued for their categorization as "white" in order to retain their property and land as naturalized citizens. In both cases, they were denied "whiteness" and lost everything.[8]

Another example of this is seen in the changes over time in how the U.S. Census Bureau has counted persons of Mexican heritage. In 1930 the U.S. Census included "Mexican" as a racial category. After protests from the Mexican government about classifying "Mexican" as a racial category, the U.S. Census in 1940 and 1950 included instructions to regard Mexicans as "white unless definitely of Indian or other nonwhite race."[9] Starting in 1980, the U.S. Census considered Hispanic origin as an ethnicity that could be from any race.[10] Though persons on the U.S. Census in 1990 and in 2000 could identify themselves as white and Hispanic or black and Hispanic, for purposes of investigation, the group of nonwhite Hispanics has continued to be seen as its own racial category.[11] This is seen in the research done on wealth disparity, in which the net worth of white families is compared to that of black or Hispanic families.[12] Persons from Cuba, Puerto Rico, Mexico, and a number of other Spanish-speaking countries are at times lumped together as "Hispanic" and at other times differentiated into separate racial categories. Because of the history of colonization, citizens of these countries have a range of skin tones, from fair to dark, representing the varied skin color of their ancestors: Spanish colonialists, indigenous peoples, and enslaved Africans.

Because our ideas about race continue to shift, using a static definition of racism may not be effective in naming ongoing problems. For instance, Mark Chesler's definition of racism as "racial prejudice plus power"[13] does not account for the subtle exchanges of power in personal interactions or the shifting nature of prejudice. It excludes the complexity of what Kimberlé Crenshaw Williams calls "intersectionality," or the ways persons can have overlapping social identities of privilege and oppression.[14] If we speak of "whites" as always being in the position of power, it is difficult to include in our conversation any examples of injustice against Jews, poor whites, non-heterosexual whites or whites with disabilities.[15] Persons in society are stratified based on a number of status markers, so speaking about "race" and "racism" as the primary way of analyzing social discrimination can seem to oversimplify the daily experiences of discrimination and struggle that persons across racial categories experience based on other aspects of their identity.

At the same time, scholars of racial theory highlight the central role of whiteness in the creation and perpetuation of racism in the United States.[16] To stake this claim is to identify whites as those who benefit from the racial hierarchy as it currently stands. Yet this creates a source of conflict for those whites who view themselves as those who are *disadvantaged* racially today. Despite statistics highlighting racial inequality in terms of wealth, health, and employment that favor whites' advantage,[17] whites report feeling they are the new targets of discrimination.[18] Researchers found that whites feel a rise in "anti-white bias," that they are among the targets of discrimination, viewing "racism is a zero-sum game that whites are now losing."[19] This sentiment is expressed in court cases that challenge affirmative action in university admissions, in which white applicants feel they have been unjustly discriminated against because they are white.[20]

Racism as a Concept Requires Conversation

Considering the different ways race and racism have changed over time, it can feel impossible to be "caught up" and "up-to-date," because society continues to change. The rise in interracial marriages means that more children and adults are biracial, and how they navigate discussions on race and racism may be different as well. Families who adopt children from a race different from their own also have unique perspectives on what is important to say about race and racism today.

All of this means that presenting definitions of race as if they are authoritative may not be the most helpful approach. Attending to the ambiguities of what we mean by race and racism requires sensitivity and a willingness to listen to the stories of others. It also means we need to continue to be aware of ongoing inequalities in how some groups are treated differently than others. While a lot has changed in society, there is still much that remains the same. White congregants living in predominantly white neighborhoods and attending white churches need to be able to listen to the ways racism continues to impact the persons of color who live and work among them. Helping white congregations think about *race* also involves helping them think about themselves as *white,* and how that racial category continues to be significant even if they feel their whiteness has given them less advantage over time.

Yet even with all of the challenges involved in defining racism, it is still helpful to have in mind what we are trying to preach against. Overall, it is helpful to view racism as an ingrained feature of living in the United States as a "racialized society," where race has been used historically to signify a higher or lower status in a racial hierarchy, where whites continue to benefit from their position in the racial pyramid, and where racial inequality persists because those in power maintain the structures that benefit them. This understanding links racism directly to the history of the United States, and though we are not the only country to exhibit racism, our particular history with racism greatly impacts how it remains in effect today. Racism is rooted in historical events and the development of race-based oppression. At the same time, racism is not just about the past but also the present realities of racialized existence and inequality. If the continuation of racial inequality is a consequence of the racial structure that benefits whites, then whites do not experience the negative impact of discrimination, and the inequality appears to be a natural outcome. This perspective on racism points to the "rational" nature of whites' resistance to talking about racism, since maintaining the racial hierarchy serves whites' interests—even though these interests are economic and pseudo-psychological, rather than spiritual and moral.

Racism also includes beliefs about the superiority of one group over another. Such beliefs emerge from the already-existing patterns of racial segregation and discrimination in which these ideas are used to justify and make sense of the racial hierarchy. For instance, whites prevented children of color from attending white schools that were better funded and staffed, providing only white children with the newest books and most current resources for learning. When black children did not do as well on standardized tests, whites did not attribute this to the lack of educational resources available to children of color, but instead developed racist beliefs about whites being more intelligent than blacks. These racist beliefs in turn have been used to justify the official or unofficial segregation of resources. In other words, racial stereotypes are based on actual racial interactions that result from the racialized structure, and are used to further justify that structure. But pointing out the injustice in the larger system means calling attention to benefits that the dominant racial group receives as a result of that structure, and challenges the meritocracy image persons in power often have of themselves. Maintaining the racial order serves the economic and pseudo-psychological interests of those who are in power. In summary, racism is not simply a matter of beliefs, but a way of justifying inequality.

Changing Assumptions about Racism

What follows are some possible ways in which white listeners may be hearing the word *racism* and what helpful interventions might be useful in your sermons or teaching to broaden the conversation for what racism means. By identifying the imaginative realities your congregants may be holding and acknowledging how the history of racism has morphed and changed over time, you will be better equipped to bridge the gap between your use of the word *racism* and what your congregants hear. Some of the perceptions you may encounter include phrases like "reverse racism," a desire to achieve a "melting pot" America, and the preference to avoid racism through "colorblindness."

However, simply telling people they need a new definition of racism does not change their perceptions, and perhaps does more damage to the relationship than to the individual's construct of racism. It is important not to view their frameworks as simple "myths" that need "debunking." It is important to recognize where people are coming from so you can be more effective in expanding your listeners' capacity to see racism in new ways.

In the book *Divided by Faith: Evangelical Religion and the Problem of Race in America,* authors Michael Emerson and Christian Smith describe common themes they have heard from white Christians concerning the meaning of racism.[21] Eighty percent of those surveyed by Emerson and Smith viewed racism as a "very important issue to address."[22] Yet, in the actual face-to-face interviews, when the white participants were asked to name concrete instances of racism, most were unable to list current examples.[23] White Christians they interviewed saw racism as a problem, but they were less sure how it remained problematic today.

In fact, many of the white Christians in the study denied that there remained a significant race problem. While most seemed to accept that racism continued to exist as a result of human imperfection, few believed that widespread discrimination still impacted racial minorities. Because they view racism as individual-level discrimination, and they do not view themselves as discriminating on the basis of race, "they wonder why they must be challenged with a problem they did not and do not cause. As they communicated to us over and over, they do not have much interracial contact, but when they do, they are friendly toward people they do meet from other races, and some even claim healthy interracial friendships."[24] If that message reflects the perspectives of members in your congregation, it will be challenging to communicate why they should be concerned about racism today.[25]

Emerson and Smith argue that this particular framework for viewing racism prevented these participants from seeing racial inequality and the significance of race in the United States today, and they highlighted three themes that emerged from their data for how whites tended to view racism. Emerson and Smith said these white Christians' understanding of racism emphasized *individualism, relationalism,* and *anti-structuralism. Individualism* includes the basic belief in equal opportunity, that persons can succeed if they work hard, and that America is a meritocracy where those who are at the top are there because they have earned their place.[26] *Relationism* is an emphasis on relationships, personal relationships with both God and others. The evil of racism, from this point of view, can be seen most clearly in the bad relationships persons have with one another. *Anti-structuralism* conveys the belief that because equal opportunity is supposedly available to all, we should resist government intervention as a strategy for addressing racism. To view social problems systemically calls into question free will individualism and challenges the core belief in freedom of opportunity. For the white Christians they interviewed, "the 'race problem' is not racial inequality, and it is not systematic, institutional injustice. Rather, [they] view the race problem as (1) prejudiced individuals, resulting in poor relationships and sin, (2) others trying to make it a group or systemic issue when it is not, or (3) a fabrication of the self-interested."[27]

Emerson and Smith include a sample interview with a 27-year-old white woman named "Debbie" who demonstrated this perspective. When asked whether the United States has a race problem, Debbie responded, "I think we make it a problem." She went on to explain that it was a matter of misinterpretation. "I feel like once in a while, when an argument happens, say between a black guy and a white guy, instead of saying 'Hey, there's two guys having an argument,' we say it's a race issue."[28] Viewing race as a problem "we make," Debbie demonstrates an individualistic interpretation of racism, viewing it not as systemic but as a problem between individuals, particularly when persons "say it's a race issue," turning a conflict into an issue of race. From her perspective, Debbie says the race problem is caused by other people who make it a problem.

Ten Myths about Racism

ʌ we view and talk about racism impacts what we feel called to do in response. Helping our white congregations see racism in different ways can expand our capacity to respond. While Emerson and Smith identified a few themes they found in their interviews with a group of white Christians, these views are not the only ones held by persons in communities of faith. Some persons in congregations are well aware of racism, that whites benefit from systemic racism, and that we need to do something about it. But even when we have the "right answers" to what racism means, we can still harbor illusions and "myths" that make it harder for us to make a difference where we can.

Consider the following myths as possible beliefs we may unintentionally harbor, as well as responses you might hear from members of your congregation, or perhaps from other people you interact with who hear you speak about racism. Understanding where people are coming from can help us better know how to engage the conversation. If we can recognize the underlying assumption, perhaps we can speak to their objections and invite them into further dialogue.

Myth 1: Racism is not our problem.

This first perspective may come across as a question. "Why do we need to talk about *that*?" The assumption is that *we*, in *our* faith community, are not racists. Helpful ways of expanding listeners' capacity to see racism as everyone's problem is to name some of the implicit biases that people may not even notice: pulling your purse closer to you when in an elevator with a black man; walking to the other side of the street when you see people of color coming your way; feeling afraid or nervous when you are around people of color; assuming a person of color must be guilty of a crime if pulled over or arrested by the police; jumping to conclusions about a persons of color stealing something from you when you may have misplaced it; needing to ask people of color "Where are you from?" meaning a different country, when you do not ask whites the same question. These examples highlight the subtle ways that implicit bias is still at work in our lives and in our world.

Another way of framing racism as *our* problem is to identify the advantages that white people may experience. In other words, name not just the negative side of the impact of racism on communities of color, but also the additive side, or the way white people have benefitted from years of racism. Activist Peggy McIntosh's article on white privilege has a lot of helpful ideas for naming those instances when whites continue to benefit.[29] Though these privileges are different for whites who experience other aspects of their identity as marginalizing, including their religious affiliation, there are enough examples that it is possible for even the most disadvantaged white person to be able to relate to at least one of them.

For whites, racism is *our* problem because we continue to experience the separation of others who cannot stand to be in community with us any longer because of how painful it is for them.[30] We are regularly reminded that our response to the sin of racism is insufficient. We have not repented. We have not tried to "go and sin no more." We have failed to adequately address the sins of former generations, and instead have defended these actions by memorializing Confederate generals in names of streets and statues. We have let our economic interests blind us to our shared humanity and the call to love our neighbors as ourselves, instead blaming people of color for poverty and decrying "handouts" for the poor.[31] Racism is *our* problem because we have yet to honor God with our response to this sin, or to build relationships with those who have been most hurt by our silence and complicity.

Myth 2: Racism is only about hateful actions and words.

If racism were only about mean things people actually say and do, then we would not need to talk about the larger patterns of discrimination that continue across the country and through the generations. If racism is just about mean actions and words, then we could easily say this is not about us; we ourselves do not harbor racist beliefs or say racist things, at least to people of color. Two problems come from this. The first is assuming that we are the best judges of whether we ourselves are racist or not; the second is that it misses a whole world of data that shows other factors in racial inequality and discrimination.

Racism is more than someone calling a person of color by a mean name. It is also seen in differences in pay,[32] in housing discrimination,[33] in mortgage lending,[34] school segregation,[35] and rates of policing and incarceration.[36] Whites may not feel that we have anything to do with these larger problems, but our silence *is* part of the problem. Our acceptance of the status quo makes these injustices harder to challenge. While racism is seen in hateful actions and words; it is also seen in our inaction and silence regarding these larger social problems that stem from our racist history and continue because of our indifference.

Myth 3: Only Ku Klux Klan members and white supremacists perpetuate racism.

It is easy to envision the "bad guys" when it comes to talking about racism. They look like men wearing white sheets and pointy hats, burning crosses in yards. We think of the images of young white men chanting "Blood and soil!" in Charlottesville in the summer of 2017. If you live in the Northeast part of the country, perhaps you picture Southerners only, not thinking about persons of color who were enslaved in the North or those who continue to experience discrimination in northern states today. If you vote as a liberal for Democratic candidates, perhaps you have in mind conservative Republicans as being the ones with the problem. If you are a Republican, perhaps you view only members of the far-right as the true racists. If you live in urban metropolitan cities within the United States, maybe you think about white people living in the country or small towns as being racist although in major cities gentrification and segregation continue to impact people of color. If you grew up surrounded by people who used the 'n-word,' maybe you can see yourself as very different from these others, since you refuse to say that word.

The moment we are able to point away from ourselves and to some other person or group as being the "real racists," we become like the self-righteous character in Jesus' parable in Luke 18, who assumes himself to be righteous and declares before God, "God, I thank you I am not like other people" (Lk. 18:11). The moment we catch ourselves making that distinction, we need to remind ourselves to be more like the tax collector in Jesus' story, asking, "God, be merciful to me, a sinner!" (Lk. 18:13). Particularly for whites, when we are faced with great opposition from other white people when talking about racism, we need to remember that we are no different *than* other white people. We share the same benefits from the sinful legacy of racism.

Myth 4: Racism has to do with our intentions.

One of the challenges of talking about racism is the assumption that for us to be guilty of something, we need to have had the intention of doing something wrong. If we have no intention of offending someone else and no consciousness of racial bias, then we may feel resentful for being accused of racism. Especially if we are generally good people who feed and clothe the homeless and give our money to the poor, it can feel as if we are being unjustly accused of racism when the rest of our behavior shows our moral intentions.

Unfortunately, great harm can come to others, not simply by our *intentions*, but by our *inattentions*. If we are not paying attention to the ways others are harmed by larger social forces that may indeed be out of our personal control, but yet nevertheless benefit us in unjust ways, our inattentiveness to these social forces can feel hurtful. Paying attention to the ways racism continues to unjustly privilege white people and disadvantage people and communities of color enables us to see racism as much bigger than our intentions. If we say something that inadvertently hurts someone else, we do not need to get defensive. Instead, we can say,

"I'm so sorry. I did not realize what that would sound like or feel like for you." We can use the experience as a learning opportunity to see life from another's point of view.

Myth 5: Racism is caused by ignorance.

By attributing racism to ignorance, we ourselves are ignoring all of the "learned" people who have argued academically for the justification of slavery and racism. Scientists have claimed to demonstrate the inferiority of other races to Caucasians by pointing out head circumference and other physiological "proofs" for the white man's superiority. Trained clergy with academic degrees argued for the legitimacy of slavery on religious grounds. Lawyers made cases for "separate but equal" schools for children of color segregated from white children. White politicians with college degrees have labeled entire countries of black and brown populations with derogatory terms. By their levels of education alone, these men and women do not qualify as ignorant people.

Even at the highest levels of academia, persons of color continue to experience racism from those who are bearers of the intellectual torch. Even in the most liberal of spaces, people of color feel the objectification of their bodies and presumption that they are less competent than their white counterparts. And among the most well-meaning and well-trained white people, persons from minority groups experience "othering" in subtle and overt ways that say to them they do not belong.

We cannot blame racism on ignorance, because we perpetuate it even when we should know better. To say racism is only about ignorance denies the ways racism has been justified and defended by persons fully aware of their views of white supremacy as well as by those who utterly denounce white supremacy and seek to work against it.

Myth 6: Racism is irrational.

This myth is related to the previous one. It assumes that racism does not make sense, and that it is based on faulty ideas about the racial superiority of whites over nonwhites. But what do we mean by *rational*? Sometimes we do not function out of a rationality based on virtue and a belief in our common humanity. Sometimes we operate out of a rationality of common sense that includes "what serves our best interests." As a white person, if given the choice to live in a good neighborhood with excellent schools for your children, where your house is likely to appreciate in value, would it not be rational for you to want to live there if you can afford it? If developers want to build apartments in that neighborhood to increase the availability of low-income housing, giving more people access to great schools, it may seem just as rational to want to protest such development; you do not want your children's schools overcrowded, the possibility of increased crime in your neighborhood, or the possibility of home values declining. These responses may all seem "rational," while at the same time perpetuating a system of racial exclusion.

The way racism perpetuates itself is often through these more subtle avenues. We take for granted the ease with which, or possibility that, we can afford to live in expensive neighborhoods, and we assume that others who cannot are less deserving. We fail to consider how our prejudices operate to preserve our own self-interests. It is completely rational for us to want the best for our children. It is completely rational to want our own home investments to increase in value. But how do we respond to persons for whom the color of their skin prevents them from buying a home in the best housing markets or getting a mortgage for a home they can invest in?

Myth 7: Racism can be remedied through education.

There is widespread belief that efforts at educating white people can actually reduce the amount of racism in the world. If only people knew... If only we heard more about this problem... If only we talked about it more and educated ourselves about racism... Surely there is an answer in one of these many books!

Unfortunately, education cannot solve all of our problems. We are selfish. Even if we know we should be less selfish, it does not make it any easier for us to want to share with others. Even if we have been educated in liberal schools, it does not prevent us from operating out of our unconscious biases. Even if we have been taught to recognize that the stereotypes about people of color are not true, we may still respond physically out of deep prejudices when we are least aware.

Some people have never had the advantages of an education, and yet have led the way in anti-racism and kindness toward all people. If we assume racism can be remedied through education, then we are assuming a privileged status for those who are educated, as if those with education are more virtuous, or at least have a greater capacity to be good. But again, you are invited to consider the people in your life who have had the least education and yet have modeled exemplary lives.

How we change is something of a mystery. Sometimes we change through experiences we have in education. Sometimes it is through a relationship with someone else. Sometimes, we feel a spiritual call to live differently; maybe we are convicted when hearing a message or something we read. But even when we feel convicted to live differently, it is another matter altogether how we actually live. All of this is to say: there is no easy answer; we have to keep working at this.

Myth 8: Racism will end as we have more and more interracial relationships.

One of the ways white Christians have tried to address racism has been to focus on integration by getting people of color to be part of our churches. This is a strategy also at work in institutions of higher learning where administrators have responded to historic segregation by bringing in more people of color to predominantly white institutions as students, staff, and faculty in the hope that such actions will increase interracial relationships and reduce racism. Certainly this has been an important step in working toward racial justice: acknowledging the history of segregation and racial inequality by making space for persons who have long been denied access.

Many cite the work of Harvard psychologist Gordon Allport with the early idea of getting people together in order to reduce prejudice.[37] In 1954, Allport published *The Nature of Prejudice,* in which he described a "contact hypothesis," the idea that more contact between groups will decrease prejudices between the two groups under ideal circumstances. According to Allport, the key qualities that need to be present in such interactions include: (1) equal status (relationships should not be between persons with different levels of power in a hierarchical structure); (2) cooperation (an opportunity for the two groups to work together on a project); (3) common goals (sharing a goal that both groups are working toward); and (4) support from social and institutional authorities (the groups should not have to meet under the stress of enforced segregation).[38] These four qualities—equal status, cooperation, common goals, and support from society and institutions—do not all have to be present for there to be a positive impact on prejudice, but the lack of equality, for instance, can greatly decrease the likelihood that the dominant group's prejudice can be reduced effectively.

Making the connection to faith communities, while it is important for our congregations to become more diverse, it will not be enough to end racism. Traci West, in her book *Disruptive Christian Ethics: When Racism and Women's Lives Matter,*[39] writes about her experiences as an African American in white congregations in which she was repeatedly told that she had a beautiful voice, though she was actually self-conscious about not having a good voice. Because she was the only African American in the congregations she was visiting, these assumptions and awkward interactions left West feeling even further marginalized.[40]

The fact that most white churches remain almost exclusively white in terms of congregational membership is problematic, recalling the words of Martin Luther King Jr.: "At eleven o'clock on Sunday morning when we stand to sing 'In Christ, there is no East or West,' we stand in the most segregated hour in America."[41] The reason our churches are segregated stems from the long history of racial discrimination, with the formation of churches and denominations based primarily on race.[42]

Are multicultural churches the answer to this problem? Returning to Gordon Allport's contact hypothesis, there has been hope that greater multiculturalism can reduce levels of racism.[43] Unfortunately, even within multicultural faith communities, there is opportunity for racism to operate. Korie Edwards, a professor of sociology, conducted a study of a multiracial congregation to see how whites and people of color negotiated their relationships and church community. Edwards found that whites continued to remain dominant in power positions in the church, even when their percentage of overall membership declined to the point of being a minority within the church.[44] In other words, racism still exists even in multicultural contexts, and it is important to keep talking about it even when we have made significant progress in becoming a more integrated church and society. Particularly for white people within these congregations, we need to continue to examine our own racism and how it may be at work even when we have a lot of interracial relationships.

Myth 9: Racism is not something that impacts my friends of color. Some people just have a chip on their shoulder and use the "race card" for their benefit.

These series of statements are part of an interrelated constellation: the basic underlying myth is that racism itself is a myth, made up to over-correct for past history and to play political mind games. This myth says racism is not a real concern, actually, but is fabricated by persons who are self-interested in what talk of racism can do for them. "If people of color that I know don't bring it up, that is another sign that it is overblown and insignificant, a secret plot by the liberals to advocate for more political correctness."

If your friends of color do not share with you their experiences of discrimination, it does not mean that it has never happened to them. There are many reasons why persons of color may not choose to share such stories with others. Even if you do not think racism impacts them, you cannot be sure. Even if your friends of color tell you it does not impact them, there are still many others for whom racism is a daily threat to their well-being. There are stories persons have been willing to share that you can access online: from famous people,[45] as well as from everyday people of every age.[46]

When someone has a "chip on their shoulder," the phrase makes it seem as if that person is disproportionately angry about something, and that they have held onto a grudge much too long. This sentiment is heard in statements such as: "Slavery ended over a hundred years ago, so get over it!" Yes, slavery ended with the Civil War, but the events that occur every day across this country remind people of color that they are still not equal, and saying slavery ended more than a hundred years ago ignores the ugly history of Reconstruction and Jim Crow laws. To accuse someone of being overly sensitive means we do not understand what it is like to live in their bodies, to go through what they experience. It is helpful for white people to sit with the discomfort of another person's pain, to acknowledge that we do not "get it," and that we have no right to tell someone when or how they should "get over" something that continues to threaten their own safety.

The third component in the series of sentiments is that people of color benefit from talking about racism—that they have a "race card" they can play to their advantage. Anne Cheng has written about the race card and its meaning for persons of color living in America who continue to feel the depressing impact that such a phrase has on persons who never feel advantaged by their race.[47] Cheng asks, "What does it mean that the deep wound of race in this country has come to be euphemized as a card, a metaphor that acknowledges the rhetoric as such yet simultaneously materializes race into a finite object that can be dealt out, withheld, or trumped?"[48] She points out the irony that the liability of race has come to stand for an asset: a special "card." To respond to this sentiment, it is helpful to highlight recent statistics about the impact of race on one's ability to secure a mortgage from a bank or pass on wealth to one's children,[49] to be shown homes one is interested in buying or renting, to get interviewed for a job, or to live a long life with access to quality healthcare—or, conversely, one's likelihood of being stopped by the police.[50]

Myth 10: Racial discrimination is against the law; what else can we do?

While racial discrimination is "outlawed," there are ways in which laws continue to enable such discrimination to take place. Michelle Alexander, author of *The New Jim Crow: Mass Incarceration in the Age of Colorblindness,* has argued that the harsh drug laws of the 1980's "War on Drugs" have resulted in the mass incarceration of men of color—prison sentences and felony convictions that have justified the same kind of discrimination allowed legally under the 1877–1950s Jim Crow laws: housing discrimination, job discrimination, and the inability to vote.[51]

There are some positive state and federal laws that have been or should be put into legislation that require greater accountability for police officers' use of deadly force. There are laws that can and do address the unequal sentencing practices and the detrimental effect of over-policing poor neighborhoods. More laws are definitely still needed. At the same time, laws will not be enough. Yes, laws need to change, as well as individuals and society as a whole. There is a lot more that needs to be done.

Politicians are still able to push through laws and policies that perpetuate racial discrimination, such as travel bans that only affect persons from majority-Muslim countries, or immigration policies that crack down hardest on Latinx immigrants and separate even young children from their families. These laws and policies are new and evolving, and yet they also resemble legislation the United States has enforced in the past. The relationship between legislation and racism is always complex and yet interrelated; we need to advocate for greater racial justice in every area of our society, and at all levels of government.

Do any of these myths sound familiar to you? The exercise of naming myths and common misperceptions about racism is meant to help us better prepare for the challenges of talking about racism in our white contexts. Awareness of the conflicting meanings that may emerge when we use the word *racism* can help us listen carefully and engage individuals at their place of concern. Myths can prove to have powerful effects and can create a strong resistance to talking about racism.

Again, the answer to these myths is not simply telling another person, "What you are saying is a myth." The answer is conversation, listening, and respect. The more we can help one another understand the complexity of the problem, the closer we can get to addressing the problem within our own spheres. Awareness of these myths hopefully can aid preachers in painting a more nuanced picture of racism in modern society, inviting listeners to see more deeply the many facets of racism that contribute to the fissures in our community.

Expanding Understanding through Empathy

Dr. David Campt is an African American speaker and author who helps groups engage in difficult conversations together.[52] In a forthcoming book, he writes about the role of empathy in helping white allies have conversations with persons he calls "racism skeptics."[53] Campt advises white allies to maintain a posture of humility when talking with racism skeptics, and to follow a method he describes with the acronym R.A.C.E., which stands for *Reflect, Ask, Connect,* and *Expand*. The first part of the process is our own self-reflection (the R standing for *reflect*). This reflection gives white allies the opportunity to consider how their own views on particular issues have changed, bringing to mind particular stories in their own lives when they believed the same things as the racism skeptic. In the second component, A stands for *ask*: inviting the racism skeptic to share what stories led them to have the beliefs they currently hold. The letter C stands for *connect*: when the work of empathy takes place. Use your own story of change to connect with the other person. Campt suggests various types of stories you can use to connect with the other person, such as sharing an "I half-agree with you" story, followed by another story that helped you think differently. This moves you into the *expand* part (the E in his acronym of R.A.C.E.), when you demonstrate how your own views have changed through a different set of experiences. These stories can help the other person see what has changed your perspective—which may not necessarily change their own point of view, but it may help maintain the relationship so that further conversations can take place.

Campt's advice can aid preachers in their work as well, using the method of connecting our own past stories to the perspectives shared by listeners in our congregations. Connecting with our hearers can help them see we have not always held the views we have now, and that we have experienced change. Witnessing to our own stories of change can inspire change in our congregations. Outside of the preaching moment, members of your congregation may also want to share their testimonies of how they came to see racism the way they do now. Perhaps you could offer time for testimony during worship, or facilitate conversations when your community is gathered together. The atmosphere of trust and relationship-building can make possible the sharing of change stories that may contradict other's views about racism.

Strategies for Naming Racism in Our Preaching:

1. Don't assume everyone is thinking of the same thing when you mention "racism." Consider when you held different views about racism than you do now.

2. Move toward the stories you hear from congregants about how they view race. Be compassionate and understanding. Try to understand how and why they view racism the way that they do.

3. In your preaching, move from story to story, expanding the frame of reference by telling stories that help listeners see a different point of view, naming stories of change that identify moments of recognition that racism impacts individuals on a broader scale.

Chapter 4

Talking about Racial Identity with White People of Faith

Our sense of identity often comes from our faith tradition. For Christians this identity is about how we have been given new life in Christ, given the ability to live as new people—brought back into relationship with God and one another—and given a new identity in Christ. Within various religious faiths, congregations often include converts, people who have converted from one tradition to another, marking their own new identity as a person in this particular faith community.

As preachers and teachers, you help your congregants live into that new identity. You show how we are called to live in community, lifting up practices of spiritual formation that shape our identity as people of faith. You preach and teach sacred texts, telling the stories of God's work in the lives of the most unlikely sinners, reassuring your listeners that God can use anybody. You point toward how our faith impacts our lives.

But how does our faith identity relate to our racial identity? Our sense of identity can be shaken when we come to grasp just how deeply we have been influenced by racism. In our congregations, some white people may have a hard time coming to identify with being white, and not resonating with this identity may make it harder for them to understand how racism continues to play a role in their own lives. In multicultural congregations, whites and people of color may differ in how significant they feel their racial identity is for them.

In her study of a multiracial congregation, Korie Edwards looked at the differences in how persons described their identity, noting that white members were less likely to identify themselves racially than the members who were persons of color.[1] These same white congregants all believed that racism continues to be a problem in the United States and that racism puts African Americans and other persons of color at a disadvantage.[2] The white congregants, while able to articulate a structural understanding of the continued existence of racism, at the same time did not view their own identities in terms of race, and did not view themselves as being particularly advantaged in society. Edwards writes, "While interracial interactions have the capacity to influence the racial attitudes of whites, they do not necessarily impact how they view their own location in the social structure and the consequences of that location. In other words, interracial interactions, for whites, do not affect the salience of their own racial identities. *Race continues to be about other people.*"[3]

If our white congregants are going to challenge racism, they need to see it as impacting their own lives, not just the lives of other people. Somehow they need to better understand how addressing racism also meets a deep need for their own spiritual growth and development. If as preachers we do not help our congregations make that connection between their racial identity and the need for becoming actively anti-racist as part of their faith identity, then they may not make the connection themselves. We need to help our congregations envision what it might look like to live into this new reality, helping them see how this new identity is connected to who they already know themselves to be. A sense of continuity is important for persons to integrate new aspects of their identity into their previous sense of self.

This sense of continuity is important not just for the individual, but for the congregation as well. Michael Emerson and Christian Smith connect church members' sense of identity with whether or not they feel comfortable in a congregation, pointing to what is known as the homophily principle. Within the current context of "church shopping," where visitors attend several different churches before settling into one congregation, persons choose to attend religious organizations that are most likely to provide a sense of meaning and belonging. This sense of belonging has to do with identity and whether a person feels he or she shares enough similarities with others in the faith community. On the negative side of this homophily principle is that members are likely to leave when they begin to feel too far on the margins of this group. For the sake of a greater sense of belonging, they will leave and join another organization.[4]

This puts a lot of pressure on you, the preacher. If you consistently veer too much from members' shared identity and their views, people may choose to go elsewhere. Emerson and Smith suggest this may be a reason is it hard for religious leaders to offer prophetic social critique. They write: "[T]he shape the laity want the prophetic voice to take is usually that which supports their own felt needs."[5]

However, I believe that preaching about racism can also be about the congregants' own felt needs. If we connect preaching about racism to the larger social context, helping our congregants identify with a positive movement toward greater justice for all, we are indeed addressing a very deep need among white congregations. Key for preachers today is helping white congregants gain a new identity, an identity that recognizes the painful legacy of racism *and* connects them to a promised redemption that includes all of God's people. It is crucial that each of us sees ourself as part of this changing identity as well; we have to stand with our congregations and journey together toward a new anti-racist racial identity.

Racial Identity Development's History and Implications for Preaching

One of the important tools I have used in my own journey of learning about racism is the concept of racial identity development theory. It has given me a framework for understanding my reactions, as well as a roadmap for where I should hope to go as I continue to learn about racism. It can also help us as faith leaders to pair our psychological development with our spiritual formation, allowing ourselves grace as we learn and grow and experience a range of difficult emotions.

Theories of racial identity development were initially developed by psychologists who were trying to help persons of color move out of internalized racism toward a more positive self-understanding while living in a racist society. Theorists later began looking at how whites develop an anti-racist white identity, seeing how whites also need to develop a revised racial identity in the midst of growing up and living in a racist society. Stages of white racial identity development include the disorienting experience of coming to an awareness of racism, an experience often accompanied by feelings of guilt and shame. Sometimes we can then project those negative feelings onto others in order to avoid feeling them ourselves. Knowledge about these stages and what we might expect in ourselves can be helpful for moving through the difficult emotions that arise.

What I found most helpful about the stages of white racial identity development was that the stages do not stop with our negative emotional reactions. Several stages exist beyond disorientation, pointing to a different way of being white in the world than I had previously imagined. When I first started doing my research, my feelings of shame and guilt over racism seemed to be the consistent result, but as a preacher I knew preaching that resulted only in shame and guilt could not be received as good news.

In following the pattern of the stages of white racial identity development, developmental theorists argue for the necessity of a *positive white racial identity, not based on illusions of supremacy*. This was a radical idea for me—that as a white person I could have a positive racial identity, which meant not feeling terrible about being white while, at the same time, continuing to acknowledge the harm of racism and actively working against it. This was beginning to feel more like good news to me.

Developmental psychologist Janet Helms is one of several theorists who developed a stage model for white racial identity development. Each stage represents a distinct "worldview," which Helms defines as "cognitive templates that people use to organize (especially racial) information about themselves, other people, and institutions."[6] These various worldviews or stages affect how persons relate to persons of other races, and the more advanced worldviews lead to a greater sense of well-being.[7]

Helms states, "The greater the extent that racism exists and is denied, the less possible it is to develop a positive White identity."[8] This means that racism and white identity development are inversely related: you cannot have a healthy sense of white identity without acknowledging the reality of racism and working to overcome its power in your own life. In order to fight racism in its many forms, Helms argues that it is critical for whites to develop an anti-racist white racial identity. Helms says this process involves both "abandoning racism" and developing a positive sense of what it means to be white. Helms states: "[H]e or she must accept his or her own Whiteness, the cultural implications of being White, and define a view of Self as a racial being that does not depend on the perceived superiority of one racial group over another."[9] Within this concise statement, Helms offers a brief summary of the development of a positive white racial identity.

Psychologist Beverly Daniel Tatum demonstrated the effectiveness of introducing students to the stages of racial identity development in enabling them to stay actively engaged in uncomfortable discussions on racism throughout a semester course on the Psychology of Racism.[10] As part of her course, Tatum exposed her students to Helms's stages of racial identity development at the onset of their discussions on racism. As Tatum discovered, understanding these stages can contribute to students' positive engagement with the process of racial identity development. By outlining the stages as presented by Helms, Tatum enabled her students to accept the emotions that came with the various stages as they identified their emotions in the process. Tatum used the students' journal responses to demonstrate that awareness of the developmental stages supported students in staying engaged throughout the duration of the semester, rather than withdrawing from the course as they were inclined, as reported by their journaled self-reflections. Tatum observed:

> The emotional responses that students have to talking and learning about racism are quite predictable and relate to their own racial identity development. Unfortunately, students... consider their own guilt, shame and embarrassment or anger an uncomfortable experience that *they alone are having*. Informing students at the beginning of the semester that these feelings may be part of the learning process is ethically necessary (in the sense of informed consent), and helps to normalize the students' experience. Knowing in advance that a desire to withdraw from classroom discussion or not to complete assignments is a common response helps students to remain engaged... [S]haring the model

of racial identity development with students gives them a useful framework for understanding each other's processes as well as their own.[11]

If knowledge about the stages of racial identity development can help students in the classroom stay engaged with the process of discussing racism, perhaps faith leaders can use this framework to encourage congregants to do the same, increasing their capacity for long-term engagement in working against racism.

Seeing the connections between the stages of a positive white racial identity and spiritual formation, religious leaders can plan thoughtfully for a long-term approach to addressing racism within their congregations. White preachers could follow the strategies Tatum advocates for teaching about racism in the classroom: create a safe climate, encourage opportunities for self-generated knowledge about racism, name the problem by explaining the complexity of racial identity development, and empower persons so that they can be agents of change.[12] Leaders' sensitivity to the often-distressing emotions that stem from the process of racial identity development and discussing racism can help inform their messages when talking about racism in predominantly white congregations.

For whites, the stages of racial identity development described by Helms and Tatum include: Contact, Disintegration, Reintegration, Pseudo-Independence, Immersion, and Autonomy. The first three correlate with the process of abandoning racism, while the second three involve the defining of an anti-racist white identity.[13] Understanding the catalysts for moving from one stage to another can help preachers in identifying possible moments of encouragement and intervention in the lives of their parishioners as they proceed through the process of white racial identity formation. Through the various stages of white racial identity development, movement to an anti-racist white identity takes multiple moments of conversion, moving from one stage to another.

Stage 1: Contact

The process of developing a white racial identity, according to Helms and Tatum, begins when a white individual first comes into contact with persons of color or the idea of other people groups who look dissimilar from the individual. In much of suburban America, the racial homogeneity of neighborhoods and racial discrimination in housing make it easy for many whites to grow up knowing few if any persons of color. Thus the *Contact* stage for them may begin very late, perhaps when they enter college or the workplace. While whites may know persons of color in their community or places of work, they may lack deep relationships where they could have heard persons of color describe their own experiences with racism.[14]

In the preaching context, it is hard to know where congregants are in their development. Some will have grown up in very different contexts: some in integrated neighborhoods, others in the segregated Deep South, and still others may have been active in the civil rights movement of the 1950s and '60s. At the same time, having a predominantly white preaching context may mean that many are at this first stage. The fact that our worshiping communities are highly homogenous testifies to the discomfort many white congregants feel toward building relationships with persons of color. It can also be seen in how the congregation markets itself—Who are the members you are trying to attract? If your church is in a neighborhood with a changing demographic, do your evangelizing efforts go toward these newcomers, or primarily to the commuters who drive in from the suburbs?

Meanwhile, it is crucial to begin in a place of empathy and solidarity with your congregation. For white faith leaders, we need to see ourselves as engaging in the process of racial identity development along with our congregants. Again, returning to the idea from David Campt (discussed in chapter 3) that we start with empathy, consider how you first experienced yourself becoming aware of racism. What did you go through that brought on this awareness? How does your own neighborhood context and where you grew up impact your earliest thoughts about race? Use stories—your own as well as other examples you can find in books or news articles that bridge the initial way you viewed race to a different understanding.

Stage 2: Disintegration

Stage 2 of the racial identity formation for whites is called *Disintegration,* because it involves a breaking-down of one's previously held positive views of oneself, feeling bad about unfair advantages gained through a racist society. Whites enter the stage of Disintegration when we go through the cognitive dissonance between how we *perceive* the state of race relations and the *reality* of racial discrimination. This process is painful; white people may feel disoriented and confused when we recognize our own complicity and ignorance about racism. It also can be very painful for white persons to become aware of the potential of microaggressions, or that much of the wealth of whites can be traced back to slavery or the exploitation of persons of color. [15]

To help listeners (and oneself) move beyond initial emotional reactions of guilt and shame, which in and of themselves are not effective in fighting racism, preaching about racism should include naming the emotions whites experience when talking about racism. It is difficult to move past these feelings if we refuse to acknowledge they are there. If we internalize a sort of self-loathing because of our own whiteness, we tend to project that negativity and judgment onto other white people who do not see racism the way we do. This cycle of judgment and self-loathing prevents positive relationships from forming that could lead to lasting change among others in your network.

As congregants begin to experience the disorienting stage of the process of learning about racism, it would be helpful to introduce the stages of white racial identity development. Recognizing they are not alone in their feelings may help them remain engaged. This is particularly important at the Disintegration stage, when our dislike for feeling guilty may turn into resentment toward those who are leading the discussion, viewing others as trying to make us feel bad for things we didn't cause. White congregants may respond with denial and/or anger when they hear a sermon that names "whiteness." You may even ask in the sermon if listeners have the urge to walk out, in order to help them identify these feelings, and invite reflection on their reactions. Laying out the stages of white racial identity formation can help congregants anticipate their own reactions to the process and help them trust that you are not trying to make them feel guilty.

In my first book, *Anxious to Talk about It: Helping White Christians Talk Faithfully about Racism,* I lift up the idea of "response-ability" as distinct from "responsibility." I have found this distinction lessens listeners' assumptions that I am trying to make them feel responsible for a racist society that they feel they did not create. I instead encourage them to focus on their own "response-ability," their ability to respond to the stories from others of how they have been impacted by racism. Focusing on our own responses can help us move away from the Disintegration stage and stay engaged in the conversation.[16]

Stage 3: Reintegration

The third stage in Helms's model is *Reintegration,* and it may create confusion when trying to talk about it. Be careful when introducing all of these stages: they are not necessarily "progressive"—and some, such as Reintegration, can actually take us backward. The name Reintegration comes from the idea that this is an experience of bringing back—or "re-integrating" into one's self-identity—a sense of pride and white innocence. In response to the negative feelings experienced when talking about racism, white people can begin to revert back to a more consciously racist point of view.

Helms says that in response to the discomfort that awareness of racism brings, white people may try to make themselves feel better in three ways: "(a) changing a behavior, (b) changing an environmental belief, and (c) developing new beliefs."[17] Examples would include avoiding future interactions with persons of color, considering current racial inequalities as a result of processes beyond your control and not something you can do anything about, or trying to find people of color who will tell you are not racist and that you are one of the "good white people." This stage describes these kinds of behavior and thinking as a predictable experience that many whites have when learning about racism, turning our negative feelings away from ourselves and onto others. This movement from Disintegration to Reintegration is a negative step, but it is an important part of the process to name since many whites experience this. It may also happen at the congregational level, or societal level. When people cannot handle their current state of anxiety, reintegrating a positive view of oneself in the social order becomes a comfortable alternative.[18] Again, this stage is not a "move up" from the previous stage, but rather a move "over" or a move "down." Developmental models may not help us climb a ladder to greater maturity, but they can be helpful in naming our experiences and finding commonalities, as well as giving us insight for how we might be able to change.

If pastors can help congregants anticipate the stage of Reintegration as a predictable but negative reaction to learning about racism, the hope is white congregants can stay engaged in the learning process, trusting that their negative feelings are not the final goal. It may not be the case that you name "Reintegration" or the other developmental stages in your sermon, but you can share stories that express the beliefs and perspectives of persons who may be in this stage. Again, leading with empathy and compassion toward your congregants in whichever stage they find themselves will provide space for them to explore their racial identity. Staying engaged in the process may depend upon whether congregants feel accepted. When talking with groups, I often admit that I do not always "get it right" or know what to say about race, and I suggest that telling ourselves we are going to make mistakes reminds us that we all are still on a journey of learning.

Stage 4: Pseudo-Independence

The fourth stage represents a movement out of Reintegration, and becoming more aware of how race functions in society. Helms labels this the *Pseudo-Independence* stage, because it shows an independence from the racist assumptions of white superiority, but only superficially. It is an initial step of accepting whiteness as a factor that shapes our political and social environment, and accepting that whites benefit from racism. Learning about "white privilege" can open our eyes to see ways we have been able to avoid talking about race because our white experiences have been considered the "norm."[19]

To help the congregation learn more about critical approaches to whiteness, your preaching can incorporate the contributions of persons of color to theology. Reading from W.E.B. DuBois and Howard Thurman, Emily Townes and Delores Williams, to name only a few, you can point to the rich history of Black theology. Drawing from the theologies of Asian/Pacific Islanders such as Chung Hyun Kyung or Hispanic/Latinx or *Mujerista* theologians such as Ada María Isasi-Díaz, you can introduce your community to the insights about God that emerge when reflecting on God's work from the margins of society. Citing the work of scholars who are writing about their personal experiences of racism can help your listeners deepen their understanding of our call to serve in the world.

At the same time, while white people are learning more about racism, there may also be the tendency to keep this work on an intellectual level, feeling reluctant to engage in real relationships with people of color. The white person in the Pseudo-Independence stage may still have doubts about whether racism is really as big or as prevalent as people say it is, wondering whether these theories of racism are too absolute and essentializing. While the white person in the Pseudo-Independence stage may feel convicted of racism on an emotional and intellectual level, behaviorally they may still exhibit symptoms of a racist system and an acceptance of the benefits they receive from it.[20]

In churches, the Pseudo-Independence stage can be seen in the regular approach to addressing racism: one-time events or studies that have no lasting impact on the congregation. Presbyterians have been known for their emphasis on educating their clergy, and I share in that appreciation for education. I love reading books, and having conversations around books can facilitate these difficult conversations. But what happens afterward? What does the congregation do differently as a result of having studied this subject? Still more is needed to help the congregation to fully engage in anti-racism.

Stage 5: Immersion

The fifth stage, *Immersion*, describes a concerted effort to learn more about racism, its history, and its current ramifications. In this stage, whites can benefit from immersing themselves in this work both relationally and intellectually. When white people learn about the history of other white people who have also worked against racism, we begin to see role models of people who look like us doing this work.[21] Immersing oneself in these stories and studying the work of people of color, whites can make connections to the larger struggle, imagining themselves taking part in the effort, identifying themselves among the many allies in the struggle to end racism and other forms of oppression.[22] Rather than focusing on helping persons of color, the white person seeks to promote awareness among other whites, perhaps sharing the stories of the anti-racist white allies who have gone on before them.[23]

A way for white communities to immerse themselves in this history is to work with other communities of faith who are actively addressing racism. Interfaith work can strengthen the sense of identity that "we are in this together," and can expand our understanding and awareness of the struggle for racial justice in our particular geographic location. Immersing ourselves in interfaith work against racism can also lead whites to see the connection between racism and other forms of oppression.

Stage 6: Autonomy

The last stage in this developmental model is called *Autonomy*, to represent the individual's ability to be distinct from previous assumptions about whiteness. This does not mean that the white person is no longer part of the racial group that continues to benefit from the legacy of racism, but it means that the white person is constantly committed to questioning assumptions of white superiority. This stage represents a holistic understanding of the work needing to be done in one's community, understanding and accepting that we will keep learning along the way. As with the other stages, this final stage for white racial identity is less an achieved status than a state of perpetual striving. Helms describes:

> Internalizing, nurturing, and applying the new definition of Whiteness evolved in the earlier stages are major goals of the Autonomy stage. In this stage, the person no longer feels a need to oppress, idealize, or denigrate people on the basis of group membership characteristics such as race because race no longer symbolizes threat. Since he or she no longer reacts out of rigid world views, it is possible for him or her to abandon cultural and institutional racism as well as personal racism... [T]he Autonomous person actively seek[s] opportunities to learn from other cultural groups. One also finds him or her actively becoming increasingly aware of how other forms of oppression (e.g., sexism, ageism) are related to racism and acting to eliminate them as well... It is a process wherein the person is continually open to new information and new ways of thinking about racial and cultural variables.[24]

It may be helpful to consider this stage as a set of goals rather than achievement. There is no such thing as a magic box you can check, saying you are a "good white person," and this final stage recognizes the futility of efforts to justify ourselves. Coming to this stage means we are perpetually open to learning more about the experiences of persons of color and fighting systems of oppression in the areas where we can exert influence. The person "no longer feels a need to oppress, idealize, or denigrate... because race no longer symbolizes threat." In earlier stages of development, whites may find themselves idealizing marginalized groups, which is another form of paternalism. Instead it can be helpful to remember that no one is perfect, that there are still problems in every community, and that we are all learning together.

Racial identity development theorists such as Janet Helms have provided us with a helpful framework for understanding the psychological process for whites coming to see ourselves as white and changing our ingrained habits and beliefs about race. Learning from one another while remembering that our current experiences are part of a process can encourage white religious leaders and congregants alike to embrace the difficult journey ahead. Working with other organizations and faith communities in our neighborhoods and cities, we can build coalitions of people of faith who are together working to dismantle racism, listening to more and more diverse voices, and identifying with a broader movement working for change.

Strategies for Preaching to Help Forge a New White Identity:

1. Offer educational opportunities for members to learn about stages of racial identity development and to hear one another's stories of being racialized a particular way. In your preaching, use stories about experiences and feelings you have gone through in your own journey toward anti-racism.

2. Build congregants' connection to a larger history of people working together for the good of all God's people. In your sermons, point out previous role models—*beyond,* say, Martin Luther King Jr., Rosa Parks, and Ruby Bridges—and including white anti-racist role models. Help listeners connect to a larger movement of people working together to end racism. Get your community engaged in building relationships with another faith group or organization working against racism. Maybe one of your members is already connected with such a group; provide space for them to share their experiences and invite others to join them. Help your listeners see that working against racism is part of our identity as people of faith.

3. Help listeners to take note of their emotions and thoughts regarding racism, and encourage them to stay engaged in the long-term struggle. Feelings around racism are heavy. They will not get easier to carry. But knowing how to care for ourselves through naming our emotions will drastically improve our ability to continue this work.

Chapter 5

Biblical Preaching about Racism[1]

So far we have focused on gratitude, the role of interpretation and recognition, ways to communicate what we mean by the word racism, and how to talk about racial identity with white people of faith. But how does that come into conversation with scripture? As preachers, you are expected to expound upon your communities' sacred texts. The act of preaching requires close attention to the holy words your congregation is entrusting you to interpret. How does this discussion of racism fit with your responsibility to illuminate the Bible for your listeners?

In his book *The Witness of Preaching*, homiletician Tom Long argues that, at our best, preachers serve as witnesses to the work of God by testifying to what God reveals in scripture.[2] According to Long, such witness requires that we attend carefully to the text, exegeting it and reflecting on it deeply, followed by testing our observations by reading what biblical scholars have to say about the text. Once we've done that, before we can move toward the sermon, we first must distill from all of that reading a *single claim* of the text upon the hearers. Once the preacher is clear about the text's claim, the next step is to write out a single statement regarding the focus of the sermon (what the sermon will *say*), and another statement stating the function of the sermon (what it will *do*).

This is a very helpful process for narrowing down the sometimes off-the-map ideas that emerge in the process of sermon creation. Having a focus of the sermon (what you want the sermon to say in light of the claim of the biblical text) and knowing its function (what you want the sermon to do or evoke in the hearts and minds of the listeners) can help you wrangle the many ideas that emerge in sermon creation to more directly relate back to the text itself and the focus and function of the sermon. I continue to recommend this method to my students of preaching; I think it helps us stay connected to the text and to be more intentional about what we hope to accomplish in our sermons.

At the same time, a challenge of this approach for preaching about racism is the direct movement from the claim of the text to the focus and function of the sermon. The focus and function statements should connect to the claim of the biblical text. But if the claim has nothing to do with racism, then how can you preach a sermon about racism that faithfully witnesses to the text?

Part of the problem in preaching about racism is that what we know of racism today was not present in the biblical text. Racism as a concept developed much later than the writing and canonization of the texts we know as the Bible. According to New Testament scholar Cain Hope Felder, "The biblical world predated any systemic notion of races and theories of racism."[3] But even if racism is anachronistic to the biblical text, the reality of racism—conceived of as a system of hierarchical racialized categories that elevated whiteness closer to godliness—received its greatest support from white Christians preaching on biblical texts. Beginning with justifications for the slave trade, white Christians have used the Bible to create and sustain racist practices and beliefs.

Another part of the problem has to do with our understanding of "*biblical* preaching." While this is a phrase that is echoed in conservative evangelical circles more often than within liberal circles, it is an important concept to consider. You may firmly believe preaching about racism *needs to be biblical;* however, what does "biblical preaching" mean, exactly?

The phrase "biblical preaching" mainly emerges from evangelical contexts. Haddon Robinson, recently deceased, was known as a primary voice of biblical preaching. He wrote homiletical textbooks that argued for expository preaching (explaining the biblical text verse by verse), and warned against a focus on applications of the text or bringing social sciences into preaching. In the tome he helped edit, *The Art and Craft of Biblical Preaching,* Robinson wrote the first entry on the "Convictions of Biblical Preaching," which I have shortened to get across the seven primary points he makes:

> To do the tough work of being biblical preachers, men and women in ministry must be committed to certain truths. *(1) The Bible is the Word of God... (2) The entire Bible is the Word of God... (3) The Bible is self-authenticating... (4) This leads to a "Thus sayeth the Lord" approach to preaching... (5) The student of the Bible must try to get at the intent of the biblical writer...* Simply put, "The Bible cannot mean what it has not meant." *(6) The Bible is a book about God... (7) We don't "make the Bible relevant"; we show its relevance.*[4]

There are several elements of these "convictions" that I disagree with, and I will go so far as to say that some of the convictions behind Robinson's notion of "biblical" preaching are not *truly* "biblical." In particular, the statement, "The Bible cannot mean what it has not meant," is a factual error. The Bible has meant, and continues to mean, more than one thing, depending on your interpretive community. To say the Bible cannot mean what it has not meant suggests a static and unilateral interpretive community.

Even within the days of Jesus' ministry, the Bible meant different things to different people. The views of the Samaritans as raised in the encounter in John 4 between Jesus and the Samaritan woman reflect different interpretive communities. The Sadducees who said there is no resurrection from the dead in Mark 12:18 again are representative of different interpretive communities. The history of the church in Acts shows different interpretive communities as Peter converts to seeing the Gentiles as included within Christ's intended recipients of salvation. Interpretation—trying to understand what the Bible *means*—is not unilateral. It is multivalent and depends upon our social context—it depends upon the interpretative habits of our communities of faith.

Different Communities of Faith, Different Frameworks for Interpretation

Biblical scholar Renita Weems writes, "How one reads or interprets the Bible depends in large part on which interpretative community one identifies with at any given time."[5] Think about the different communities you have been a part of: How do you read the Bible when you are part of a small group of laypeople reading scripture together? How do you read the Bible while in a seminary classroom? How do you read the Bible when you are with a group of other pastors or teachers? Weems continues:

> The average reader belongs, in actuality, to a number of different reading communities, communities that sometimes have different and competing conventions for reading and that can make different and competing demands upon the reader... For in the end, it is one's interpretative community that tends to regulate which reading strategies are authoritative for the reader and what ought to be the reader's predominant interests.[6]

If you are part of a community of faith that interprets scripture by focusing on the original intention of the author, then perhaps you may never consider elements of the text that have any connection to our current understandings of race. The original intention of the author may not have been to talk about race, since race as an ideology was not yet in existence. However, there are other interpretive communities who share this passion for biblical preaching and yet who *do* name the evils of racism. This includes Hispanic preaching contexts, Asian American preaching contexts, and African American preaching contexts.

In their book *Púlpito: An Introduction to Hispanic Preaching*, Justo Gonzalez and Pablo Jimenez demonstrate examples of how scripture has been interpreted in different Hispanic contexts.[7] Gonzalez points to the community-centered nature of biblical interpretation: "When I open the Bible in order to begin preparing a sermon, I fully expect, not just to discover in the text something I had not seen before, but also to see all those around me and myself under a new light. Biblical interpretation is not ultimately about the text, but about the community in which the interpretation takes place, and which in turn is interpreted by the living text."[8] In light of that community, González points to some of the factors impacting Hispanics that, in turn, influence his preaching and interpretation of the Bible: the challenges of living in a United States where one is still treated as an outsider, the constant assumption that one is an "immigrant" even if one's family has lived in the area longer than that area was considered part of the United States, and a constant message of devaluation—one which says your language and culture are inferior.[9]

In a chapter on Hispanic hermeneutics, Jiménez writes that there are three basic ideas about scripture that several Hispanic biblical scholars have pointed to: the Bible is liberating, the Bible enables a reading of resistance that challenges the current social order, and the Bible points toward an eschatological vision of judgment and hope.[10] In light of this kind of reading, Jimenez suggests a paradigm for interpreting scripture using the following model: first, by looking for the places of marginalization in the biblical text as an entry point; second, by seeking points of contact between one's community and the text; third, by making a correlation of social locations between the characters in the story and members of one's community; and fourth, by finding a key metaphor to help communicate the liberating gospel to the listeners.[11]

Asian American preaching contexts also present particular interpretive communities for reading the Bible. In *Preaching the Presence of God: A Homiletic from an Asian American Perspective*, professor of homiletics Eunjoo Mary Kim describes some of the challenges facing Asian American faith communities. Kim points to the "model minority" stereotype of Asian Americans, citing a 1982 *Newsweek* cover with this phrase, which presents Asian Americans as the image of the successful immigrant. Kim reveals the harm of this stereotype: Asian Americans, as the "model minority," are seen as "good" for assimilating into white culture and not threatening the dominant white society. This sends a message to other groups of minorities that they are less successful because they have failed to assimilate and adopt white cultural values. Kim also points to how the model minority myth makes invisible the many Asian American men and women who are still struggling economically and with language barriers, constantly seen as "Asian" rather than "American," and judged more harshly for failing to meet the higher expectations set by the model minority stereotype.[12]

According to Kim, within Asian American communities, biblical interpretation serves as a source for spiritual guidance. She writes:

The Bible is the preacher's intimate partner in guiding the community of faith along its spiritual journey. The Bible is the source of creating a new vision for the future of the community of faith. The preacher...experiences the presence and power of the Spirit from the text and at the same time calls forth the experience of the congregation in order for them to listen to the will of God.[13]

Connecting the spiritual traditions of the congregation to the life-giving Spirit that speaks to us through scripture, Kim provides an image for how Asian American contexts shape the preacher's interpretation of the text.

African American preaching traditions also have let the biblical text define the sermon, as well as allowing the concerns of the community—particularly the painful realities of racism they experience—impact how the Bible is interpreted. The lived experiences of the congregations are the context for interpreting the Bible in preparation for preaching. Homiletics professor Cleophus LaRue emphasizes: "More than a mere source for texts, in black preaching, the Bible is the single most important source of language, imagery, and story for the sermon."[14]

LaRue doesn't define biblical preaching in as narrow or specific a set of convictions as Robinson. LaRue writes, "In many black churches, biblical preaching, [is] defined as preaching that allows a text from the Bible to serve as the leading force in shaping the content and purpose of the sermon..."[15]

The Bible shapes the sermon in black preaching traditions, and there is still room for naming the sin of racism that impacts so many persons within those interpretive communities. Homiletics professor Frank Thomas identifies this form of reading as "existential exegesis," a way of reading the text with the human situation clearly in mind: "African American preaching operates from the perspective of a close observation of the Bible and human need, which directs the sermon to resolve existential concern by exegesis of the text."[16] At the same time, different interpretive communities within black churches have interpreted the text differently over time and in different contexts.

Biblical scholar Vincent Wimbush has outlined five different movements over time within the history of African American biblical interpretation. At the beginning of the African experience in North America, enslaved Africans noticed the impact of the Bible on their European captors. Wimbush writes that the initial reaction among many Africans was one of rejection, suspicion, and awe for what they saw as the "Book of Religion" held in such esteem by the whites. In the 18th and 19th centuries, when the Great Revivals were taking place in the North and South, enslaved Africans were converting to Christianity in great numbers. In particular, the evangelical movements of the Methodists and Baptists conveyed a message of direct experience with the Bible and faith, encouraging a view of the

Bible as accessible to all, including slaves. White evangelists preached to slaves and exposed them to the Bible in new ways. Wimbush identifies this period of African American interpretation as the emergence of the Bible as a "language-world," a shared language in which they could interact with one another and with whites on a different plane than that of their current social context. The bible as a language-world enabled enslaved Africans to inhabit a shared language with one another at a time when white slave owners had often intentionally thwarted their ability to communicate by separating people from the same tribe so they could not speak to one another. However, in the words and stories of the Bible, the slaves could enjoy a form of communication that they shared, a story they could live into and identify with, that differed from the story they were told about themselves by whites.[17]

In the fight for the abolition of slavery, the Bible was claimed as a resource for freedom as well as a tool for the hypocrisy of whites. David Walker, an African American abolitionist in 1829, argued that white Americans do not believe the Bible when they fail to love their black neighbors as themselves. This period of interpretation in the black religious tradition marks the emergence of a distinctively oppositional hermeneutic to the way white pro-slavery apologists used the Bible.

Wimbush says that the most recent trend in African American biblical interpretation is fundamentalism. He links this with a sense of crisis in the black church. While fundamentalism in the white church can be linked with the crisis of consciousness brought about by the scientific revolution in the late 19th and early 20th centuries, fundamentalism among African Americans has emerged in many ways in reaction to the "inadequacy of culturalist religion," as Wimbush describes it: "Buttressing this perception [of the inadequacy of culturalist religion] is the assumption that anything distinctively black is inadequate in the dominant white world."[18] As a result, some African Americans have moved away from black churches and into white fundamentalist churches.

So in the context of understanding *biblical* preaching, there has been the desire in white evangelical circles, as well as some African American communities, to see as "true" biblical interpretation that which is devoid of racialized language or cultural interpretive references. For white evangelicals, this may be because they have not seen race or racial oppression as a central part of their experience of faith. For black evangelicals, some may see an emphasis on black experience as insufficient to help them succeed in the dominant white world.

At the same time, as seen in the works of González and Jiménez, Kim, and LaRue, preaching within contexts of Latinx, Asian American, or African American congregations continues to incorporate biblical texts with the lived experiences of racial discrimination. Our different contexts impact how we read the Bible, and our experiences of race impact how we see the

Bible relating to our lives. For those who insist that preaching be *biblical*, it is important to show how our reading of the Bible is always situated and embodied.

What's "Biblical" about "Biblical Preaching"?

While racism continues to exist and infect our communities of faith, naming it as evil is necessary, and focusing simply on the original intent of the biblical authors is not always sufficient for helping us to address this evil. Other methods of biblical interpretation and approaches to understanding its meaning are crucial for helping us to expand our ways of viewing the Bible as a liberating source for *all* of God's people, including whites and other persons in dominant social positions. This means changing some of the ways we approach the Bible and our expectations for our interpretation. Looking back to some of the claims by Robinson for what constitutes biblical preaching, it is important to push back and re-examine some of his assumptions.

First, to require a commitment to the meaning of the author's original intention, if that were even possible, is to force the reader to separate from her or his own life situation. Wimbush writes of how setting up strict rules for interpretation can cause one to miss out on how the Bible speaks to persons in their everyday lives, and that a focus on authorial intent "necessarily forces a certain delimitation and qualification of questioning and probing. It forces the interpreter to begin not in his or her own time... but in another one—that (one that is imagined or assumed to be) of the text."[19] This is problematic, particularly for persons who remain at the margins of society, who hold the least amount of power. Again, here's Wimbush: "There are high stakes in such practice for peoples on the periphery. At the very least, it keeps them distracted, unable to focus on their world situation."[20] For this reason, Wimbush spends time focusing directly on the experience of African Americans living in the United States.

Robinson's conviction that biblical preaching must only mean what the text *meant* can also cause problems when we notice the harmful social structures present during the time the Bible was written. The original intentions of the authors should not necessarily be preached today. For instance, slavery existed during the time of the New Testament writings, and the biblical authors do not speak against it as a practice, a factor cited by proslavery preachers who argued for the justification of slavery on biblical grounds.[21] New Testament scholar Mitzi Smith identifies where the ideology of slavery appears in problematic ways in the synoptic gospels as well as in John, in which Jesus' parables contain images of slaves as disposable and the "locus of abuse."[22] And even in instances in which slaves were freed, the problematic difference in power was still present because even freed persons were never truly equal to those who were freeborn in the Roman world. This hierarchy was maintained, keeping freed persons always subjugated to the will of the freeborn Roman citizens. These social patterns were not questioned within the parables of Jesus related by the gospel writers, nor by authors of the epistles. If we read these texts and go with what the authors originally "intended," then we may be interpreting the texts in ways similar to white Christians of the 19th century who defended slavery as an institution, or who saw nothing wrong with the practice and so did not trouble to preach against slavery.

Biblical scholar Clarice Martin demonstrates how black slaves and proslavery whites had very different interpretative approaches to these texts. Martin points out that Charles Hodge, a Presbyterian theologian and professor at Princeton Seminary in the 19th century, used these biblical texts to argue for slavery in writing about the Fugitive Slave Law.[23] Additionally, legal courts cited scripture when an 1829 judge argued that cruel battery of slave women was not illegal since the master's will had to be obeyed, as by the "law of God."[24] Among the texts cited to defend oppressive racial hierarchies were the "household codes" found in the Bible, in which slaves were told to obey their masters and wives to submit to their husbands. Rejecting the original intentions of the authors, enslaved African Americans knew that when white slave owners preached about slaves being submissive, they were *not* proclaiming the gospel of Jesus Christ. Slaves may not have been able to read the Bible, but they knew these texts were not from God.

While African Americans rejected this interpretation of the household codes as they related to slavery, Martin points out that black women continued to bear the weight of the household codes' injunctions against women in leadership.[25] Early 19th-century black women preachers Julia Foote and Jarena Lee[26] both had to resist the interpretations of these biblical texts that suggested women "learn in silence with full submission," and were not "to have authority over a man" (1 Tim. 2:11–12). They lived into their calls to preach, but faced strong resistance from others within the black community. Still today, many black women (as well as women from other racial groups) face challenges to their ministry because of these texts.

Biblical Preaching: Being "Biblical" *and* "Contemporary"

John Stott, an evangelical author and leader from the 20th century, wrote, "The characteristic fault of evangelicals is to be biblical but not contemporary. The characteristic fault of liberals is to be contemporary but not biblical. Few of us manage to be both simultaneously."[27]

This characterization is something I want to contest. I want to argue that evangelicals *can* be biblical *and* contemporary when preaching about racism, and liberals *can* be contemporary *and* biblical, particularly when it comes to preaching about racism.

Here are two examples of pastors who are already doing this. On the evangelical side, Rick Richardson makes the case in his essay "Cross-Cultural Preaching" in the same anthology edited by Haddon Robinson, that preachers need to be aware of the history of slavery and the evils of the Middle Passage. He writes, "As a white person, when I preach in a black context, the baggage from all that evil [of the Middle Passage] lingers. I have to show I am aware of that or I cannot be trusted... The trust issues are immense, and only people willing to recognize the evils of the past can even be heard."[28] On the more liberal side of the homiletical spectrum, William Willimon insists that preaching on racism be biblical, and that the preacher must focus on "theology rather than anthropology" in his book *Who Lynched Willie Earle? Preaching to Confront Racism.*[29]

So how can we be "biblical" about our biblical preaching, highlighting the current factors negatively impacting our faith as individuals and as communities, while drawing from the rich legacy of a faith tradition that proclaims salvation for all? Below, let me suggest ways that we can read the Bible while remaining aware of the constant danger of its misuse. Here are seven statements, corresponding to the seven assertions from Robinson's essay about biblical preaching, offering an alternative to his perspective:

1. Biblical preaching believes that the Bible is authoritative because it is the text that tells us about Jesus Christ, God in-flesh, who came to redeem all of humanity, in our flesh, and to redeem humanity from all our ways of devaluing the image of God that is found inscribed on each and every human body.

2. Biblical preaching sees all of the Bible as having the potential to be used for harm, even turned into something demonic, since the Devil himself could use scripture to try to tempt Jesus. So the words of the Bible must never be seen as unequivocally good, but as potentially harmful when used the wrong way.

3. Biblical preaching respects the Bible as a collection of writers who came from different interpretive communities and who could never have anticipated being put directly in conversation with one another. We have this canon because members of interpretive communities through the millennia have found in these texts the message of salvation, a message that comes through different voices and finds resonance in the lived experiences of believers today. Because of this, the Bible does not speak in "one voice," and is not "self-authenticating," since there is not a single "self" represented by the Bible. Faith in God requires a trust on our part that sometimes God speaks to us through scripture, and sometimes God wants us to speak up and *speak back to* scripture.

4. Biblical preaching never says, "Thus sayeth the Lord," as though preachers could unmistakably speak for God, but prayerfully hopes that God's message of love and hope and redemption may come through the work of preaching.

5. Biblical preaching requires that students of the Bible learn the history of interpretation, of how certain texts have been used harmfully, in order to address these harms in the current era lest these harms are perpetuated in the preacher's own words.

6. Biblical preaching believes that the Bible is a book about God's work to redeem humanity, which never stays in the past but always continues into the present. This requires that preachers attend to current forms of oppression and evil that flourish in society today.

7. Biblical preaching believes that words are powerful, but that the power of the Holy Spirit is what makes preaching effective in the lives of its hearers.

These seven tenets of biblical preaching do a better job of communicating that biblical preaching is *hard*. It is not easy. It is always ambiguous. And yet, it is *necessary*. Our current contexts are changing constantly. We cannot set our hopes on particular theories or social analyses as saving us. Only God can do that. And the Bible that has been handed down to us from generation to generation is a testimony to the power of God to work and redeem even though this same Bible has been and can still be used to do great harm.

When we see and hear about the harm of racism that continues to this day, we must be able to find words to say that challenge racist ideology and point to God's redemption. Rather than waiting until the next major event on the news that highlights racism in action, preachers need to bring to the foreground the way our communities have been malnourished in our own biblical interpretation by ignoring the contexts in which we live our faith. As I preach before predominantly white congregations, I keep in mind that the context for my biblical interpretation is the legacy of centuries of biblically sanctioned racial violence and oppression that has buttressed our community while devastating the communities of others. We are also descendants of white people who courageously sought to interpret the Bible differently, who used scriptural texts to preach the gospel to persons whom society deemed unworthy of conversion, and who later used these texts to defend the abolition of slavery and the civil rights movement. There is no monolithic "white interpretive community," just as there are no monolithic communities of Hispanics, or Asian Americans, or African Americans. Different communities of white people have interpreted the Bible differently over time, depending on their context. It is important that we take our own current context seriously, seeing in it the need to address racism in our society, in our culture, and in our communities of faith.

From the seven tenets that I set forth above, there are questions that we can bring with us to our reading of the biblical text as we try to be more faithful in responding to racism.

First, the authority of the Bible comes from its power to point to God's redemption-in-the-flesh of all of creation, so we ask ourselves: Where is the authority in this particular text? Where is God calling attention to the God-in-flesh redemption of all of humanity made in God's image? What does this text say to counteract the messages persons hear that devalue their particular bodies or identities?

Second, we remember that all of scripture can be harmful as well as salvific, so we ask ourselves: How can this passage be interpreted harmfully? How can it be read as good news? What is the history of how this text has been read in communities of faith, and how can it be reimagined for today in a way that brings life instead of death?

Third, acknowledging the multiple voices presented by the biblical writers, we ask ourselves: Whose voices dominate in this text? Whose voices are silenced in this text? If we imagined God empowering those silenced voices to speak, what would they tell us? Are there people silenced in our communities of faith today or in our neighborhoods? How does this text speak to different communities of interpretation?

Fourth, we remain humble about our ability to speak for God, aware of the painful legacy of religious traditions whose claim to speak on behalf of the Divine has in truth separated persons from experiencing the love of God. Aware of our limitations, we ask ourselves, as we interpret this text: How may I still be getting it wrong? Being mindful of our call to draw all persons into God's love, we wrestle with the text like Jacob at the crossing of the Jabbok (Gen. 32:22–32), wrestling with the text and saying: "I will not let you go until you bless me!" We hold on to the text, knowing that the Bible has been used harmfully in the past, but insistent that it still has power to speak truth and life to our situation today, listening for the voice of God that still speaks love and healing into our broken world.

Preaching Biblically about Racism When Responding to Crises

In addition to thinking through the questions above, the "recognition" framework can be a helpful structuring tool for bringing together the themes and messages of the sermon, particularly when preaching about racism in the aftermath of national crises related to racism. The *cognition-identity-gratitude* movement of recognition can be a helpful interpretive framework for putting racism in conversation with the biblical text.

For example, July 14, 2013, was a Sunday. The night before, the news came out that George Zimmerman had been acquitted. The year before, Zimmerman shot and killed Trayvon Martin, a young black teenager walking home in a hoodie with a bag of Skittles and a can of sweet tea. Zimmerman had followed Trayvon under the assumption that he "looked suspicious," and within minutes of calling the police to inform them of his suspicions, Zimmerman had shot and killed Trayvon. The news of his death sparked national outrage, and President Obama expressed empathy with Trayvon's parents, saying, "If I had a son, he'd look like Trayvon." The tragedy around this unjust killing led me to believe that Zimmerman would be convicted of murder. Why should any child *die* because he "looked suspicious"?

The news of Zimmerman's acquittal came late on a Saturday night. I woke Sunday morning and learned of the verdict on social media, shocked by the acquittal. My sense of faith in the justice system was rocked, even though I had been studying the history of racism for several years by that point. How could a jury *not* convict a man of *anything* after he knowingly followed a teenager for looking suspicious and shot him? Trayvon never had a chance, carrying on him only a bag of candy, a can of tea, and the heavy mark of racist stereotypes.

I did not want to go and preach that morning. My sermon, already prepared, was on the good Samaritan (Lk. 10:25–37), the lectionary text for the day. The church where I was going to preach was new to me, since I was serving as "pulpit supply," and I would not know how that congregation would be responding to this news. But I could not preach the same sermon I had already prepared, now that Zimmerman had been acquitted. Still, with less than two hours before the service, and a drive ahead of me to get there, what other option did I have? I did not have time to sit down and re-write it.

I got in my car and drove, and with the ideas of the recognition framework percolating in my mind, I reflected on what I might say on this text that could speak some message of good news. Thinking about the three-fold process of recognition, moving from cognition to identity to gratitude, I walked through the sermon with the news of the Zimmerman acquittal. I re-envisioned the first part of my sermon, thinking about cognition: How can this text help us understand racism? I decided to draw parallels between the death of Trayvon Martin and the person who "fell into the hands of robbers" in Jesus' story of the good Samaritan. By identifying Trayvon with this character, I was able to compare different responses to his death to the responses of the characters in Jesus' story. I "updated" the two characters who passed by the man left for dead by the side of the road by robbers: these were the local police, who came to the defense of the "robbers" instead of the injured man, and the media, who focused on "stand-your-ground" laws and pictures of Zimmerman's injuries to show the "robbers" acted in self-defense. I called it the "anti-Samaritan story" because it was not a "good Samaritan" who finally came to Trayvon, but the justice system as a whole, which instead came to the aid of the "robber" of the young man's life and took pity on *him,* and not the man left dying by the side of the road. They dressed *Zimmerman's* wounds and expressed concern for his safety, returned his gun to him, sent him on his way, and, eventually, acquitted him of any sin.

The second movement in the recognition framework concerns identity, so I invited the congregation to consider how we are called to act as neighbors to those left by the side of the road. I referenced Martin Luther King Jr.'s analysis that the biblical story of the good Samaritan does not just call us to charity, but to rebuilding the Jericho Road, meaning that we are to evaluate the systemic injustice and racial profiling that enabled such a tragedy to take place. I then asked the congregation to consider themselves as the robber within the story, likening the robber not only to Zimmerman, but also to us as a society. I wondered with the congregation how *we* have contributed to this tragedy by supporting programs and laws that put people at risk along the Jericho Road, or how we continue to act on our stereotypes and prejudices. I asked us to consider ourselves as the robbers so that we might know it is not just this one person, Zimmerman, who we should see as guilty despite the court's ruling, but that all of us are implicated in a larger system that relies on the fear of black and brown bodies to justify racial profiling and police brutality in order to keep whites "safe."

However, I knew I could not stop with this movement, based on the three-fold framework of recognition. I had to find gratitude in the story. I had to interpret the text in such a way as to connect with my own expression of gratitude. In my preparation for the sermon, I had read a commentary on the text from Augustine of Hippo, a theologian from the African continent, who viewed the story, not as a moral tale about helping others, but an allegory of the work of Christ in coming to save our sin-sick souls. Augustine interpreted the good Samaritan as the only one we could truly call "good"—that is, God-in-the-flesh. This good Samaritan stands in for Jesus, who sees us by the side of the road and who comes to us with healing balm of grace and new life. I connected this to the current situation by declaring that God in Christ has come to heal the wounds we have inflicted on others, that it is God who comes to comfort the mothers of black and brown boys, mothers whose fear of letting their children go from their arms has only increased since the verdict. But it is God who has gone before us, who is already working to rebuild the Jericho Road, who comes to heal our souls sickened by racism. I proclaimed that Christ is working to bring about God's kingdom, God's neighborhood—where all are safe, welcomed, and cared for. Following an expression of gratitude for what God has done and is doing in Christ, I ended with Jesus' words at the end of the text, when he asks the lawyer, "Which of the three…was a neighbor to the man?" to which the lawyer responds, "The one who showed him mercy." At this, Jesus tells the lawyer: "Go and do likewise" (vv. 36–37).

Ending with the text here offered listeners an opportunity for expressing their gratitude for God's grace in acts of mercy for others. The call to "go and do likewise" is not motivated out of obligation, but comes out of the journey of having recognized ourselves as implicated in the story, and yet forgiven by the grace of God in Christ. To "go and do likewise" then becomes an opportunity to express our gratitude to God and to one another, motivated by that gratitude to change a system that continues to target black and brown bodies.

This sermon helped me put into words a response to the Zimmerman acquittal. As a visiting preacher, I did not know this congregation, so it was hard for me to gauge whether the acquittal was even on their radar. I give this synopsis of my rapid recrafting of a sermon based on the good Samaritan to demonstrate that a three-fold hermeneutic of recognition for whites preaching on racism really *works*. It works in the sense that it can enable white preachers to put current social events that reveal the problem of racism in conversation with the biblical text, providing a clear trajectory through which to move the sermon in order to help us communicate the reality of racism, our complicity in it, and present gratitude as the proper starting ground for our work in the world.

Strategies for Biblical Preaching about Racism:

1. Remember that how we approach sacred texts is already impacted by our racialization. Consider how society racializes you, and reflect on how that makes a difference in your biblical interpretation.

2. Ask yourself: How do different interpretive communities read this text? What are the resources you can access to learn about the views of other communities? Who are the authors you turn to for biblical commentary?

3. Consider how this text may have been used harmfully in the past. Does its past misuse deserve mention in your sermon? What might you say to honor the voices of those whom this text has harmed?

4. Reflect on current events that demonstrate racism, and ask: What does this text have to say to the present situation? Does this text offer us any gifts of hope and redemption today?

Chapter 6

Theology for Preaching about Racism[1]

Before seminary, I could have easily identified racism as "sinful," but I could not have said how racism negatively impacted my spiritual life. I didn't see myself as a racist, nor did I fully understand the pervasiveness and long-lasting power of racism. And yet, as a Christian, I have theological language to address both of these aspects: naming my spiritual condition as impaired by racism, and acknowledging the difficulties of ridding ourselves of racism as a society. The theological language for understanding racism both personally and societally is *sin*.

As a Christian, I grew up with strong sin language and memorized verses such as "the wages of sin is death, but the free gift of God is eternal life in Christ Jesus our Lord" (Rom. 6:23). In high school campus ministries, "sin" was mostly a reference to sexual promiscuity or underage drinking. Racism was never discussed as a sin or as a larger system of sin. But if you had asked me if racism was sinful, I would have said "yes!"—though I had no idea that *I* was guilty of the sin of racism, or how the larger society reflected the brokenness of the sin of racism.

We need to refamiliarize ourselves with the language of sin. Theologically, sin points to the fact that what is wrong with the world is not simply bad actions, but a deeper brokenness that impacts our relationships with one another and with God, reflecting a *spiritual* brokenness. While I know "original sin" language is not popular and no longer a widely held belief, the idea that the sin of racism is inherited and passed on to our children seems to make sense.[2] Others have described the far-ranging effects of sin in terms of "fallenness"—to say that we are not *inherently bad*, but that all of humanity has *fallen* into sin, and that sin reveals itself in various forms of oppression.[3]

Theologian Rita Nakashima Brock wrote about sin as "damage" or "brokenheartedness," to point to the pain that all people experience when our relationships suffer: "sin is a sign of our brokenheartedness, of how damaged we are, not of how evil, willfully disobedient, and culpable we are. Sin is not something to be punished but something to be healed."[4] Speaking about sin in ways that point to how we have been harmed as a whole human family can help us move away from the shame and guilt that sin-talk has fostered in the past, instead moving toward a more life-giving and hope-filled longing for healing. Naming racism as sin in ways that highlight this brokenheartedness at the center of our human community can encourage us to seek God's healing and pray for our community's restoration.

Caution: Beware of Sinning in Our Sin-Talk

While naming racism as "sin" is a crucial contribution we can offer to secular discussions of racism, I want to echo a word of caution before we dive into helpful metaphors for understanding racism as sin. First of all, talking about sin may not prevent us from continuing to sin. Again here is Rita Nakashima Brock: "The acknowledgment of our sinful nature and dependence on divine power have not stopped the church and Christian nations from creating some of the most oppressive societies in history."[5] Plenty of sermons about sin came out of the mouths of preachers who endorsed the Crusades, or anti-Semitism, or slavery.

Secondly, the ways we talk about sin can actually perpetuate harm. Theologian Stephen G. Ray Jr., looking at the problematic ways sin has been discussed by theologians in the past, has argued that our discussion of sin can inadvertently perpetuate injustice against others.[6] For instance, early-20th–century theologian Reinhold Niebuhr, despite his work for economic and racial justice, depicts the "Negro" and the "Negro's cultural backwardness" in his writings in ways that repeated the racism he sought to work against. Ray says the problem with Niebuhr's logic is that "it renders the sins of marginalized persons as having a distinctly different character... [H]e discusses *the Negro's* status as a sinner as being qualitatively different from that of white Americans."[7] Niebuhr wrote about the oppression of African Americans in ways that suggested their salvation could be found in transcending their cultural background and joining white Americans' culture. Niebuhr seemed to suggest that while whites needed to transcend the evils of racist discrimination, African Americans' redemption required transcending their "backwards" and deficient culture.

Ray points out that Niebuhr was presenting a monolithic and stereotypic image of black communities that had been presented as a way of justifying segregation. Ray suggests Niebuhr was influenced by the work of Gunnar Myrdal, whose book Niebuhr reviewed in 1944.[8] Myrdal's representation of the "Negro problem" presented black communities as being the source of their own oppression. Under a subheading of "The Negro Community as a Pathological Form of an American Community," Myrdal described the "social pathology" that affects the "Negro community," negative effects he attributes to the pressures of "caste."[9] Myrdal called Negro culture a "distorted development, or a pathological condition, of the general

American culture," linking this culture to social ills including "the high Negro crime rate" and "personality difficulties."[10]

Myrdal's take on "the Negro problem" is damaging and paternalistic. The rhetoric invites the reader both to condemn this "culture" (presenting African American culture as a monolithic thing, rather than a multitude of cultures) because it demonstrates "social pathology," and to feel sorry for those who participate in such culture since "for the most part... [these aspects were] created by the social caste pressures." Ray's analysis of Niebuhr and Myrdal's work calls our attention to the way the "sin-talk" surrounding racism can in fact perpetuate the sin itself by coupling a condemnation of "racism" with a racist paternalism, a subtle way of condemning the cultural differences of nonwhite groups while evoking pity for their oppressed condition.

Ray's discussion of these authors reminds us to remain humble in our sin-talk. Particularly for whites preaching about racism, we need to be careful that we do not present persons impacted by racism as deficient in some way or deserving of a paternalistic pity. We need to be sensitive to how words and stories we use to depict racism can simultaneously perpetuate harmful stereotypes. The "sins" of sin-talk regarding racism include pathologizing nonwhites in the process of discussing injustice against them, creating a paternalistic or condescending tone toward such groups, and minimizing the problem so as to make the problem more about these other nonwhite groups than about us and our white listeners.

Another challenge in preaching about racism is to avoid essentializing all white people, describing whites' sinfulness as having a distinctly different character to that of nonwhites. For many whites who are aware of the intersections of oppression they experience—their gender or sexual identity, their ethnic or religious identity, their age or class position or experiences with unemployment or disability—all of these other experiences can make white listeners feel defensive when racism as sin becomes a monolithic label for which all whites bear guilt and responsibility. Many whites bristle at talk of "white privilege" for this very same reason. They may have plenty of reasons to demonstrate their own lack of privilege, and so the posture of our listeners becomes one of defensiveness rather than open-hearted engagement.

One way to avoid this essentializing of white people is to help our listeners see the sin of racism as it impacts all people, even when we have not intentionally been racist. Sin is not just about our own actions, but also about the impact of unjust systems that result in broken relationships. The three metaphors that I describe below can be applied to the harm all communities experience because of racism. Just as I want us to avoid assuming racism is only a problem for people of color, I also want to avoid talking about racism as only a problem for whites; *all of us* are harmed by racism. Helping our listeners join together in learning about the effects of this sin can be a more helpful approach to expanding our awareness of how all of us are harmed and impacted by racism, and how God in Christ is working to redeem all of humanity.

The critiques of Stephen Ray also remind us that talking about racism can actually contribute to racism, unknowingly committing sin while engaging in sin-talk. Naming racism as "sin" is a crucial task of preaching, and at, the same time, we must continue to be open to how we may be unintentionally harming others, acknowledging the limits of our perspective and the reality of sin that impacts us all.

Finally, I want to say that white faith leaders should never, ever, ever, *ever* use the "n-word." The word stands for *so much* violence—using it as a white person evokes all that history of terror and trauma. And that hurt is still there, so do not sin by using words that have been used to harm the marginalized, even when repeating the words of someone else. When you have conversations about racism in your church, ask white members not to repeat the "n-word," even when recounting what they were told as children. Just as you would omit curse words you did not want to repeat, treat the n-word and other derogatory terms as the offensive slurs that they are, and do not give them air time.

Three Metaphors for Sin:
Idolatry, Estrangement, and Bondage

In preaching, it is helpful to connect our understanding of racism with theological language that is already familiar to our listeners. Theologians throughout Christian history have used metaphors for sin and redemption by looking at the current experiences of people in order to, as theologian Delores Williams puts it, "use the language and sociopolitical thought of the time to render Christian ideas and principles understandable."[11] In our preaching, we can extend listeners' understanding of racism through theological metaphors for sin: *idolatry, estrangement,* and *bondage.*

Idolatry is as old as the Ten Commandments as something prohibited by God. *Estrangement* conveys the impact of sin on our relationships: sin estranges us from God, from others, and from ourselves. *Bondage* is more controversial. The apostle Paul used language of being a slave to sin in his letters, while bondage also directly connects to images of slavery, which is a central component of the legacy of racism in the United States. To use a phrase in interracial contexts that implies white people are in any way "in bondage" may strike some as offensive, since whites do not share the experiences and stories of descendants of enslaved Africans or enslaved Indigenous peoples. But the sin of racism has impacted whites and people of color by continuing to bind our minds and bodies to the ideals of white supremacy.

The question of how God relates to the struggle for racial justice has been answered in this country and around the world by volumes of contextual theologies of liberation. Many great theologians are writing from the perspectives of Latinx or Hispanic theologies, Asian American theologies, African American and Womanist theologies as well as Native American theologies.[12] Below, I lift up the voices of some of the theologians who have impacted my own thinking about theology and racism, who have written about racism as sin in ways that echo the themes of idolatry, estrangement, and bondage.

Racism as Idolatry

Some of the earliest work done on racism in the field of theology was by George D. Kelsey, a professor who taught theology to Martin Luther King Jr. In 1965, Kelsey published his work *Racism and the Christian Understanding of Man,* in which he identifies racism as idolatry, calling this idolatry an "alternative faith system." Throughout his book, Kelsey contrasts the *racist* perspectives on humanity, equality, sin, and redemption with the Christian understanding of such doctrines.[13] Kelsey writes: "The racist self, which identifies itself with wisdom and virtue, must be confronted by the Christ who is, in truth, wisdom and virtue."[14]

The "idol" of racism assumes that whites are the source of truth and the bearers of virtue. When white people turn only to other white people for knowledge, advice, wisdom, and guidance, they are idolizing whiteness as a symbol of truth, a marker that the one who is white is the bearer of truth. Assuming that whites are the ones with authority, the ones in charge, the idolatry of racism turns to whites first as the ones who hold the answers to life's questions. When hiring practices or mortgage loan officers favor white candidates over equally qualified candidates of color, the idolatry of racism elevates whiteness to a symbol of superiority. It can be a subtle idolatry, without the obviousness of genuflection or outright praise of whiteness, but it can appear in the everyday interactions we have with one another.

As I was going through airport security early in the morning recently, I noticed a pattern of whites who were trying to skip ahead in line because their flight was close to departure. The line was exceedingly slow; it took nearly an hour for me to get through, so I understand the sense of urgency and panic that some travelers may have felt. But here is what I noticed: a young white couple who were worried about missing their flight went to a white person ahead of them to ask if they could cut in line. From there, they kept walking to the next white person in line to ask permission, passing over several travelers of color. There were two young Latinx men in line, and an older Asian American. None of these passengers were asked if they could be passed in line. Not 15 minutes later, the same scenario occurred once more. A white woman with her two children asked white people in line, going ahead and quickly moving beyond the people of color in between. The fact that this happened twice made me think about white exceptionalism. These white travelers could have accepted they would need to be bumped to another flight, they could have told themselves to arrive earlier to the airport next time, or they could have purchased an upgrade "TSA pre-check" or other expedited way through security. Instead, they pushed ahead of other travelers, not asking permission from fellow passengers except from those who were white. Did these white people feel that their needs were greater than others? That their tight connection mattered more than the impending departures of other travelers? "Idolatry" includes this unquestioned assumption that, somehow, whites' experiences are more important and pressing than the experiences of others.

The idolatry of racism "sees" white people but overlooks or treats persons of color as invisible. With the idolatry of whiteness, persons who do not represent white standards become invisible. Ralph Ellison's *Invisible Man,* published in 1952, presents this experience of invisibility in a profound novel, in which the protagonist declares in the prologue, "I am invisible, understand, simply because people refuse to see me."[15] Another author with the name of Ellison, Gregory C. Ellison II, wrote in 2013 about African American young men who continue to experience invisibility, and how this lack of being seen renders them "cut dead, but still alive."[16] Invisibility can also figure into how we read the Bible: biblical scholar Clarice Martin writes of how experiences of marginalized persons are often overlooked in the scriptural narrative, even in biblical scholarship, such as when scholars have said the ethnic or national identity of Ethiopians referenced in the Bible should be discounted as "inconsequential."[17]

Mujerista theologian Ada María Isasi-Díaz wrote of the experience of Hispanic women who experience "invisible invisibility," which is when persons from the dominant society "question not only the value of our specificity but the very reality of it. Most of those who totally ignore us do not even know they are doing so; they are not even capable of acknowledging our presence."[18] Isasi-Díaz instructs persons who want to show true respect to embrace and engage Hispanic women in their difference rather than denying that we "see you as Hispanic," that people try and enter their world and understand their struggles, and together analyze the power structures that continue to render some members of the community as invisible.[19]

The idolatry of racism values the perspectives, contributions, and institutions of white culture, while simultaneously disrespecting, disregarding, or simply overlooking those of nonwhite cultures. To name the sin of racism as idolatry is to shed light on the arbitrariness of such cultural standards, standards that some members of our society "worship" by giving them full authority. To call it idolatry is also to identify its all-encompassing nature. To worship an idol is to assent to a particular worldview that holds that idol in high regard, accepts its judgments as true, and fears its wrath when transgressing its values. Both persons of color and whites can idolize whiteness, with people of color internalizing the values of white supremacy in order to survive in a racist society. At the same time, persons of color as well as whites can *resist* the idol of white supremacy, and can celebrate the beauty and wisdom of other traditions as an act of iconoclastic resistance.

In preaching about racism as idolatry, it is important not only to call attention to the idolatry of whiteness but also to lift up what worshiping the *true* God entails. Loving God with all our heart, mind, and strength, and loving our neighbor as ourselves, means opening ourselves to experiencing deeper relationships with one another. Destroying our idols means that we also tear down our protective barriers, allowing ourselves to listen deeply to ourselves and to others.

For many white people, it may feel stressful and anxiety-producing to imagine developing a close relationship with someone they fear will call them a racist or express anger toward them. Returning to Rita Nakashima Brock's understanding of sin as damage and brokenheartedness, if whites anticipate being the source of others' brokenheartedness, they may feel defensive, which may also be a remnant of our idolatry wanting to keep us immune from the pain caused by racism.

If you encounter this kind of resistance in yourself or in your listeners, remember who it is that we are seeing when we turn from our idols and turn to the one true God: we are viewing the face of a God who loves us and cares for us, even in the midst of our anxiety and fear. Even as we fear the pain of others' stories, worried that we may have caused some of that pain, we can rest assured that even in this difficult space, God is there. God is there in both the peace and the discomfort, the acceptance and the resistance, the pain as well as the gratitude. Letting go of our idols can be painful, but it can also be liberating, giving us opportunities to learn and to grow in ways we had never before imagined.

A few years after George Kelsey published *Racism and the Christian Understanding of Man*, theologian James Cone published his revolutionary work *Black Theology and Black Power*, where he boldly proclaimed: "There is a need for a theology whose sole purpose is to emancipate the gospel from its 'whiteness.'"[20] Cone argued that we needed to understand the radical concreteness of Jesus Christ as a poor, oppressed Jew, who Cone declared was *black*. Because blackness has been made to stand for everything that is wrong with the world from the white perspective, to identify Christ with the oppressed is to identify Christ with blackness. Cone later wrote about the significance of Christ's identifying with black experience during the years of slavery and lynching: "Christ crucified manifested God's loving and liberating presence *in* the contradictions of black life—that transcendent presence in the lives of black Christians that empowered them to believe that *ultimately*, in God's eschatological future, they would not be defeated by the 'troubles of this world,' no matter how great and painful their suffering."[21]

If we or our congregants react negatively to the idea that God is black or brown, or we cannot tolerate an image of a Christ who appears Latinx or Asian, perhaps we can interrogate our own reactions: Why is this offensive to me? What does this say about my own idolatry of whiteness? How does this make me feel about my own skin color? It can be helpful to give listeners the chance to reflect on whatever reactions they have to hearing God described in ways not typically associated with white cultural norms. In the pulpit, turn to theologians whose images of God reflect the diversity of God's good creation, helping listeners see God in new ways through the perspectives of Latinx, Asian American, Native American, African American theologians, and other theologians of color from around the world.

Pay attention to the physical depictions of Jesus in your place of worship. Are the pictures in your sanctuary of a white European Christ? What about the images in your stained-glass windows? What does Jesus look like in your children's Bibles or the books in their Sunday school classrooms? How do we understand the physical body of Jesus Christ as he would have appeared to others in first-century Palestine? What if our images of Jesus' family, fleeing from Herod, looked like an immigrant family from Latin America crossing the border to escape from terror? Celebrating the beauty of all bodies, all shades of skin color, and recognizing each person as made in the image of God, listeners may be more likely to see in one another and in persons who look different from themselves, bearers of God's image.

Racism as Estrangement

Another way of naming racism as sin is through the metaphor of estrangement. The sense of estrangement permeates not just individual relationships between persons of different races, but also whole communities and cultures. Racism results both from the structures of society as well as individual interactions, and naming the sin of racism as estrangement points to large-scale examples of segregation as well as more personal dynamics of isolation and interpersonal conflict.

The metaphor for sin as estrangement helps convey the alienation we experience not only from one another but from God. Sin as estrangement locates the heart of sin as separation from God and others, which results from our own actions as well as the actions of others. Estrangement is not something we *do*, but something we *experience* as a result of the brokenness of society. To speak of estrangement as *sin* is to locate it specifically within a religious tradition that confesses a transcendent God who desires to be in relationship with us, and who wants us to be in relationship with one another. Estrangement is an interpersonal and societal rupture, as well as a rupture of the divine-human relationship.

Theologian Willie James Jennings writes of the impact of racism on intimacy—our intimacy with God as well as with one another. Jennings describes that Christianity should be a faith that helps us to join one another across our differences, but instead our history has shown a tendency to oppress and dominate. Ideally, Christianity is "a faith that understands its own deep wisdom and power of joining, mixing, merging, and being changed by multiple ways of life to witness a God who surprises us by love of differences and draws us to new capacities to imagine their reconciliation."[22] Unfortunately, as Jennings points out, "[T]he intimacy that marks Christianity is a painful one, one in which the joining often meant oppression, violence, and death, if not of bodies then most certainly of ways of life, forms of language, and visions of the world."[23]

One effect of this estrangement was the loss of a deep connection between people and the land. Jennings points out that with the dawn of colonization and slavery, European Christians no longer viewed their identity through the lens of belonging to a land or to a home country.[24] As a result, they made whiteness into their source of identity, meanwhile separating themselves from the rest of God's good creation. When members of society have assumed that *whiteness* is what makes one closer to God, estrangement ruptures the unity of the creation God declared "good."

The disconnectedness and segregation we continue to experience in society are in direct contrast to the communal nature of the Trinity. Theologian M. Shawn Copeland discusses how persons created in God's image were intended to be in relationship with others as a reflection of who God is: "Humanity in its diversity is a reflection of the community of the Three Divine Persons. Their divine love constitutes our unity in and realization of the mystical body of Christ… In the mystical body, we belong to God and we are for one another."[25] Racism and oppression have led to a disruption of this unity, resulting in estrangement from one another and from who we are meant to be in community with the Triune God.

Racism also causes us to become estranged from ourselves. Racism disrupts how we view ourselves by creating a silo around our self-identity, unable to view ourselves from the perspectives of others (if we are white), or apart from whiteness (if we are people of color). Theologian J. Kameron Carter describes how racism creates a one-way transmission of identity, in which whites look only to other whites for knowledge of self, and persons of color are confined to receiving their self-identity through the racist gaze of white supremacy. This harms both groups by limiting their ability to receive knowledge of themselves from God. The history of racial oppression has led to a "one-way expression of ecstatic identity as whiteness," in Carter's words, in which whites and people of color experience alienation from God and from others through an inability to receive their identity from anywhere else but the lens of whiteness.[26] This leads to estrangement not only in society, but within individuals themselves.

Carter draws from the work of seventh-century monk Maximus the Confessor to talk about this idea of identity. In this ancient theologian, Carter finds resources for understanding how Christ heals the estrangement enacted by racism by reopening humans to one another and to God. Carter explains:

> ...Maximus conceives of human nature as being reopened in Christ, not simply to God but also to itself. Christ reopens humanity to embrace the many that is constitutive of created human nature and of creation itself. In this sense, Christ reintegrates human nature, enacting it no longer with an order of tyrannical division but, rather, in an order of "peaceful difference," the one-many structure of creation... [Christ enables] the reopening of human nature itself so that it is no longer hermetically sealed in upon itself within a "fortress mentality." For the insularity of human nature is the ground of tyranny...
>
> Maximus saw in Christ the solution to the many violent and tyrannical divisions that could arise... In Christ, the gesture of ecstatic openness to God in human self-fulfillment, which is the gesture to receive oneself from God, is necessarily a gesture of openness to all created beings as revealing God. "To be" ecstatically is to receive oneself from other human beings precisely as the receiving of self from God. Hence, being named from God entails being named from other human beings. In undoing whiteness as a theological problem, Christ leads human nature out of this disposition.[27]

In conversation with Maximus the Confessor, Carter shows how Christ heals the estrangement resulting from racism by opening up persons to one another and to God, enabling a person to receive "oneself from other human beings precisely as the receiving of self from God." When we turn to one another, we receive ourselves, uniting ourselves to persons out of the unity with God that Christ has enabled.

By naming the sin of racism as estrangement, we point to the harm we experience as a result of centuries of racism, harm that limits our ability to connect with others as well as limiting what knowledge we can gain of who God is calling us to be. Through Christ, we can be reopened to one another, building relationships and intimacy with persons who have been separated from us through racism. By reconnecting with one another across racial divides, opening ourselves to the hard conversations that healing and building of trust require, may we become a community that more closely reflects the communal nature of God.

Racism as Bondage

We may recognize the ways we have idolized a standard of whiteness in our cultural, intellectual, and aesthetic preferences, and perhaps we are aware of our estrangement from others, from God, and even from ourselves. But to name the depth of the problem of racism, we need to acknowledge how it has impacted our very bodies, even below our conscious awareness. The embodied nature of racism leaves persons habituated in immediate reactions to persons of other races, physical responses to the bodies of others that depend, not on our rational intention, but the ingrained and inherited tradition of racism. We may begin appreciating other cultures and developing deeper relationships across our differences, but how do we account for the ways we continue to speak and behave in ways that perpetuate racism? One way is to identify the impact of sin on our own bodies through the metaphor of sin as bondage.

This third metaphor for naming sin—bondage—focuses on the seeming intractability of racism: how persons respond to others out of the embodied *habits* cultivated by living in a racist society. Naming the sin of racism as bondage can help describe how even well-meaning whites *perform* racism through our bodies and in our language. Persons of color continue to experience whites' negative reactions to their nonwhite bodies, even if these negative reactions are subtle and nonverbal. Racism as bondage also points to the legacy of white supremacy, which has left not only an imprint on whites but in the internalized oppression of persons of color. This embodied quality of racism, the internalized psychological harm experienced by people of color and the reactionary habits of white people, cannot be undone by a simple rejection of racist beliefs. We cannot set aside habits this deep and ingrained through our good intentions alone.

Augustine of Hippo, the fourth-century theologian from the African continent, spoke of sin as a self-forged chain: a chain whose links we first forged, and that keeps us in bondage.[28] Understanding sin this way helps us connect ongoing racism to a past history that continues to impact the present. Racism is a human construction: it is not natural or biological. Humans created it. At the same time, though humans created racism, it is not easy for humans to simply destroy it. It lives on in us, habituated in our bodies, and entrenched in our institutions.

Racism as bondage calls attention to the embodiment of sin and the harmful stereotypes attached to particular bodies. Throughout the history of racism, white people have fostered a fear of people of color, justifying cruel treatment or discrimination by appealing to the need to protect themselves. Even if we know in our minds that people of color are not any more dangerous than white people, how do we account for the ways our bodies sometimes react with fear when we encounter persons with brown or black skin, if not by naming it as sin? Thinking of racism through the metaphor of bondage helps us attend to how we unwillingly respond to the bodies of others.

A friend of mine, a white woman pastor living in the Northwest, shared with me the following story. She was sitting in her car with the windows rolled down, parked across from a ferry landing on the Puget Sound, enjoying the sounds of the ocean and smell of salt water. As she sat there, a black man walked by. Without thinking, her hand immediately went to lock the car doors. Because the windows were down, the sound of the "clunk" of doors locking echoed loudly. The man slowed and turned to her, shaking his head with recognition, saying: "I'm not going to hurt you, lady." My friend was so embarrassed, knowing that locking the car doors sent a message to this man, a message he heard loud and clear, insinuating: "You are a threat." The fact that the man said something to reassure her meant that this has probably happened to him before. My friend apologized, saying, "I know—I'm sorry about that," but the damage was done. The physical habits of racism that teach whites to be afraid of people of color return in reflexes whites cannot control, and such reflexes continue to harm people of color. Racism is a form of bondage etched into our bodies through such reflexes, and through the embodiment of "race" as "threat."

In preaching about racism through the metaphor of bondage, the message needs to come across that such bondage means living in fear and missing out on the opportunities to see God at work in the world around us. This bondage to fear needs to give way to a new set of habits, such as active reflection on our reflexes, praying for God to free us from our fears, and trusting that "perfect love casts out fear" (1 Jn. 4:18). Cultivating the habit of love, the habit of trust, the habit of gratitude for the faces of persons you see: these habits can help us live into the freedom that God calls us to experience.

Racism as bondage refers not only to the habituated fear of whites responding to the bodies of others, but also to the ways bodies of persons of color today continue to bear the meanings and associations developed by years of racism. Michael Eric Dyson, a sociology professor as well as an ordained minister, retold a story that his daughter had shared with him. She is fair-skinned, so she often is not seen as black. One night she was walking home when she heard a man walking behind her, talking loudly on his cell phone, and she was able to tell he was black. Recognizing the vernacular "Nah, Bruh," she felt at home and at ease. But moments later, when she took a turn down another street, a white man ran to her with his arms flailing to warn her that there had been a black man walking right behind her. Dyson writes: "She was doubly irritated. The man didn't realize that she's black. And most annoyingly he believed the black man's skin immediately made him a suspect."[29] Dyson's daughter replied: "Yeah?!... He had to be a threat just because he was walking, breathing, and black?"[30]

As Dyson and other persons of color are consciously aware, this experience is more than annoying; it can be deadly: "such fear is what gets black folk killed."[31] Interpreting some bodies as threatening means that these same bodies will become targets. Professor of communication Kumarini Silva, reflecting on the 2012 shooting of six American Sikhs while they were in their temple, wrote: "Longer than a decade after the terrorist attacks of September 11, 2001, their deaths were tragic proof of the ongoing hatred toward a composite, unidentifiable brown threat."[32]

We cannot deny that racism has attached meaning to particular bodies, marking them with oppressive meanings, but neither can we consent to the power of racism nor the habits of fear. Instead we must acknowledge the marking of bodies while at the same time calling upon the One into whose marked body we have all been incorporated. M. Shawn Copeland writes of the ways these markings are taken up into Christ, illuminating how the bondage of racism must be healed by an embodied and marked Christ.[33] Reflecting on Christ's body as "marked" helps us see the markings of all bodies as part of the body of Christ, where each human body has also been marked by Christ. Our bodies are reinterpreted in Christ's body as we live as the body of Christ. Christ identifies with persons whose bodies have been marked by society, and in Christ these markings are transformed as we see them re-*membered* as Christ's body: "If theological reflection on the body cannot ignore a Christ identified with black, brown, red, yellow, poor white, and queer folk, neither can it ignore reflection on 'the flesh of the Church.' For as Gregory of Nyssa tells us, whoever 'sees the Church looks directly at Christ.' And as the flesh of the church is the flesh of Christ in every age, the flesh of the church is marked (as was his flesh) by race, sex, gender, sexuality, and culture."[34] Copeland does not minimize the ways our bodies are marked, but rather says that these markings are taken up into Christ and become the very vision of Christ in the world, reinterpreted by his cross. Therefore we do not need to erase our difference in order to be united; we are not one body in Christ because we are all the same. We are united in Christ because of the particularity of his incarnation, taking on the markings of an embodied poor Jew living under the Roman Empire, and, finally, receiving the shameful marks of crucifixion—which he still bore after resurrection. Because Christ has born these marks and continues to bear them, our physical markings are incorporated in him, which is to say, in the very person of God.

Instead of moving toward "color-blindness," in which we pretend to not see color, Copeland points out that these very identifiers are now part of what it means to be the body of Christ. The different ways our bodies are marked make all of us part of the "mystical body of Christ," linking our vision of future redemption to the concrete embodied experiences that connect us to one another: "To think of our human being in the world as the mystical body of Christ retunes our being to the eschatological at the core of the concrete, reminds us of our inalienable relation to one another in God, and steadies our efforts on that absolute future that only God can give."[35] Though the sin of racism has marked human bodies for the purposes of oppression and bondage, God in Christ resignifies the differences among our bodies as part of the beautiful body of Christ resurrected and alive in the world.

Finally, speaking of sin as bondage reminds us to attend to the emotional, psychological, and physical toll that racism takes on human bodies. As we pray for God's redemption, we need to take seriously the embodied healing that needs to take place. Rita Nakashima Brock writes that such healing takes place when we open ourselves to our deep feelings and memories: "We begin to heal, in remembrance and forgiveness, by allowing anger to surface, by reconnecting to our deepest, most passionate feelings, feelings grounded in the rich complexities of our full embodied experience, and by actively reclaiming memory, memory grounded in our relationships."[36] These relationships also enable our bodies to connect to the embodied experiences of others, enabling our healing to take place alongside the healing of others by listening to the stories that others have to share, and such sharing "binds us to the suffering of others and provides us the routes to empowerment and self-acceptance. Such memory also makes us hungry for collective memory, for the stories of our own people, and of the truth of the life of the human species."[37] Through deep, connected, embodied knowing and sharing of stories, we become more aware of the stories of the wider human family, creating a desire in us for the healing of all people.

Because the sin of racism is enfleshed in habituated bodies and embodied as markers that leave some persons targeted for violence, it is not easily overcome. Redemption and healing are mysterious and often elusive. However, what these theologians help us to affirm is that God will not leave us in our idolatry or estrangement or bondage. The hope of Christian faith is that the in-breaking of God's Spirit will continue to heal us from sin, draw us together into the body of Christ, and free us from habits of fear to live our lives out of new habits of love and embrace. Opening ourselves to this process of redemption will open us to new experiences and connections with one another, uniting us amidst our beautiful differences into relationships of compassionate sharing and growth. As we preach about racism, we point our listeners to the depth of the problem as well as the great hope we have through faith in Christ, extending the invitation to live into the mystical body of Christ in the world.

Strategies for Theological Preaching about Racism:

1. Name racism as sin through different metaphors to help listeners understand racism as more than individual acts, and connect it to a larger view of society as harmed through sin.

2. Draw from the work of theologians who have connected racism to the malformation of theology and identity, to help listeners see that racism is not separate or distinct from Christianity, but has been developed through Christian history and even justified with Christian theology.

3. Use theological concepts to describe racism, and then point to theological reasons for faith and hope. If we acknowledge the sin that continues to have power over us, we can also proclaim the good news of faith about the power of God's love over sin and death. Let the theological messages of faith be resources for addressing the theological problem of racism.

Chapter 7

Strategies for Preaching and Beyond

Each preacher has his or her own working style: some may plan out their sermons weeks in advance, some may begin early in the week, and others may leave the task of sermon preparation to the day before. Whatever your style, the ways you think about race and racism will come across in your preaching. I hope the ideas presented so far can help you think through how you live the preaching life within a racist society, giving you tools for how you can interpret scripture differently, how you can understand what different meanings the word *racism* brings up in the minds of your hearers, how the sin of racism impacts us spiritually, and what kind of personal transformation needs to happen in each one of us so we can work toward an anti-racist identity as people of faith.

What is the process for preparing sermons that address racism? In what follows, I will be asking questions for you to consider and providing sermon forms that may be most conducive to this type of preaching. In addition to these preaching forms and prompts, I want to suggest ways for you to engage your congregation beyond the pulpit. The work of anti-racism is constant; we will not be able to say we are "done" working against racism any time soon. Keep in mind the long view; we've got a lot of work to do. If you do not already preach regularly about racism, this is the week to start.

Getting Started: Questions to Ask in Preparation

As you sit down to write a sermon, what are the first things you think about? Have you already chosen your text? What is the liturgical season or nearest holy day? What is going on in the news right now? What is going on in the life of your community?

As I write this, I am sitting in a waiting area as my car gets an oil change. The television is on loudly in the corner, and the news is announcing details about a local shooting. It is hard to concentrate. Commercials come on and try to sell me cars. I cannot think about the subject at hand; phrases from the television enter my consciousness and prevent me from finishing sentences in my head.

There is a lot that competes for our attention as we prepare sermons. So much is going on in the world, locally and globally, while the forces of daily life press in on us and distract us: a bridge collapses, another political transition takes place in Washington, celebrities are caught in scandals, another storm heads our way—all in addition to the family in your church who just lost a son, the member newly diagnosed with terminal cancer, the friend from home whose dad died unexpectedly. As a faith leader, what guides your sermon preparation?

Remember that how you interpret the text is already impacted by your racialization in society. How society has racialized you is already a factor in how you approach sacred texts: either you do not have to worry about your race because you are seen as white, or you are reminded of your race on a regular basis and experience the dangers inherent to living in a racist society. So before you even go to scripture, if you are white, the challenges of recognizing racism and recognizing yourself as white are already at work, making it difficult for you to see in scripture any connection to issues of race.

It doesn't mean that these other things are not important: our communities need us to care for them in times of personal crisis. But offering care and comfort does not have to be distinct from a larger effort to engage your congregation in anti-racism work. Sermons still need to address our congregants where they are, but they should point to a future God is calling us to.

So before you even go to the sacred text to begin your preparation, spend time in prayer. Ask God to give you insight into how the scriptures can speak into the realities of living as white people in a society that gives us unfair advantages. One of the prayers I wrote about in my first book was a prayer of self-compassion.[1] The prayer helps us notice the discomfort we may feel in talking about racism, reminds us of our connection to others through shared humanity, and imagines God's love flowing over us—evoking gratitude for the work of God in us. Beginning with a prayer of gratitude reminds us that we go to scripture, not to beat ourselves up or to guilt our listeners, but because we are thankful for the living Word that continues to speak to our human condition. Start with a prayer of gratitude before you even read the text, and let your gratitude for God's love guide you as you read.

Now that you have the text in front of you and you are feeling gratitude for God's ongoing work in the world, take time to read the scripture text for yourself. How does the passage speak to you, in your own life? Continue by imagining how this passage speaks to persons in your congregation. How might this text speak to the situation in which your congregation finds itself, in a world that is growing more diversified amidst a history of racism? What issues are you all struggling with as a congregation related to how you approach discussions of racism? If you serve a white congregation, remember that they may have a hard time recognizing racism, recognizing themselves as white, and recognizing that being predominantly white as a congregation may prevent them from seeing racism clearly. Your congregation may be missing out on the gift of a new testimony to God's work in the world, simply because of its racial homogeneity or blinders. What gifts of relationship and community could your congregation be experiencing if it was willing to consider how race continues to impair our ability to love each other? Do these ideas resonate with anything you are reading from the sacred text?

Once you have read the text and have taken notes on your own reflections in response to some of the questions above, consider your personal library and go-to set of resources for preaching. Is there an Internet site you turn to for articles or ideas? Is there a commentary on your shelf for your text?

Now, take a step back. Who sources your resources? Are they people of color? Do they resemble the people in your pews, or do they offer a different vantage point? If not, how can you gain access to a more diverse set of voices and perspectives on your text? The Internet has a wide array of theological and exegetical resources, enabling us to read the text from different points of view even if we do not live close to a theological library. One such resource is the African American Lectionary, from which five years of lectionary resources for various special days and holiday celebrations are available and accessible (www.theafricanamericanlectionary.org).

Return to your initial set of reflections on the text. Has reading the perspectives of scholars from other racial backgrounds had any effect on your initial assumptions about the text? What are you noticing about the similarities or differences? What makes you feel grateful when reading the views of scripture from scholars from different perspectives? What is the good news in the text for your congregation? Write down a summary of your thoughts on the text and see if there is a focus and function emerging.[2] Do you already have in mind what the sermon will say? Do you know what response you want your listeners to have in listening to your sermon? Keep in mind the importance of gratitude and finding a way to link challenging conversations back to a sense of feeling thankful.

With the text in front of you, and an idea for your focus and function statements, remember the three challenges of preaching about racism: recognizing new meanings for racism, helping white listeners recognize the impact of race on their own identity, and motivating hearers to respond out of a sense of gratitude. While in some sermons all three components may be present, in others you may only be able to include one or two. Consider how the focus and function of your sermon can respond to one or more of these challenges.

In helping the congregation recognize other meanings for racism than what they may already have in mind, consider telling stories from literature or the news that demonstrate a challenge to the myth(s) you want to address. It may be helpful to specifically name the "common sense" understanding that you are challenging in order for your congregants to see the connections made between what they believe or may have heard, and consider what kind of response might more adequately represent the realities of racism today.

A Word of Caution

We can perpetuate harmful stereotypes even in our efforts to do good. Consider carefully the illustrations and stories you tell that call attention to race. Could any be construed as stereotypes? One of the ways we can create stereotypes in telling stories about race is to put people of color in a perpetual status of victim. Do our stories constantly highlight misfortune or injustice people of color experience? For instance, a bad way of interpreting Acts 8:26–40, in which Philip talks with the Ethiopian eunuch, is to make an analogy between our call to evangelize and going to other countries to help them understand the good news. We may not be trying to reproduce harmful stereotypes, but we may be echoing a history of justifying colonialism, ignoring the long history of African Christianity, and casting persons of color as the perpetual "outsider" in need of our help.

Instead of presenting communities of color as always in need, be intentional about telling stories in which the primary actors are people of color living their faith in powerful ways, thriving and making a difference in the world just as any other member in your congregation. While we do not want to idealize people of color either, it is important to provide your congregation with positive examples of people of color acting as agents in the world and making a difference—not just for communities of color, but for all of society.

This also connects with another caution: do not make sermons concerning racism only about people of color. Remember the second challenge, that of helping white congregants recognize themselves as white and needing to work through their own racial identity to move toward becoming anti-racist. If all the stories we use in our sermons are about people of color experiencing racism, then we may not be communicating to our white congregants that this is relevant to them. We need to also share stories of white persons who have come to see their own complicity in racism, what their moment of conversion was like, and how they are now living into a new anti-racist identity.

Perhaps as a sermon illustration or in an adult religious education setting, you could talk about the history of racism in the United States, showing how different people have been racialized differently across time.

Also, look for ways to introduce perspectives from other faith traditions. Is there a Jewish leader in your area who can talk to the experience of being racialized as Jewish and experiencing anti-Semitism? Or, a Muslim who can talk of anti-Muslim racial profiling? Perhaps members of your community can talk of their own family stories, remembering "Irish Need Not Apply" signs in store windows when Irish were not seen as "white." This gives persons the opportunity to reflect on how their own ideas of race and racism have changed over time. Reflecting on how their own views and society have changed over time, persons can better envision how society still needs to change.

Pay attention to the kinds of responses members of your congregation may have to your preaching. Be gentle with yourself and with others; each person is coming to this conversation from a different place and a different story. Expect to hear from persons who feel this is not a subject to talk about, as well as from others who are thankful you brought it up. This may also lead to follow-up conversations with members of your congregation who want to share their own stories with you of how they came to see racism in society. Consider your own process of racial identity development, and be open to ways you need to continue to grow and deepen your commitment to anti-racism.

Preaching involves not just raising awareness of issues that affect our society, but also how those same issues relate to our faith and what we believe about God, and how racism must be seen and named as sin. It is important that, as you bring in stories and talk about racism in your sermons, you also highlight that racism does not only impact people of color. Racism impacts our own relationship with God. For those of us who are white, we have made the false god of whiteness into an idol, with standards set by white people. Racism estranges us from the human family, separating us from the community of faith that is meant to be *one body*. Racism also estranges us from God, preventing us from seeing God in the faces and lives of people of color, so we miss out on the communal nature of who God is and who God created us to be. Finally, racism has marked our very bodies with sin. Black and brown bodies have been marked by racist associations with being a "threat," and white bodies retain embodied habits of fear, responding to the bodies of people of color as dangerous. Such habits separate us from the mystical body of Christ, which incorporates all bodies that have been marked by oppression. In your preaching, demonstrate that racism is a *theological* issue, one that deforms our spirits and hinders right relationships with God and one another.

Putting It Together: Sermon Forms and Frameworks

Sermon forms do not sound very exciting, but they can be very helpful in making sermons more effective. They can also give us guidance in the sermon preparation process. For instance, after you have all of your ideas down on paper, the awareness of different sermon forms may help you decide how to rearrange your ideas so they flow better, create a more logical argument, and/or present a more aesthetic experience for the listeners. Likewise, if you are in the writing mode and are not sure what you need to say next, a sermon form or framework can serve as a road map to prompt you for what should follow.

Eunjoo Mary Kim, in her book *Preaching the Presence of God*, describes a "spiral form" for a sermon.[3] Rather than the linear three-points-and-a-poem form, or other linear progressions, she describes preaching as walking around slowly, gradually coming closer to the central point, without going there too quickly or directly. This form of preaching relies on the intuition of the listener, in which connections and recognition occur, not by direct instruction, but through indirect means. The "aha!" moment for listeners may happen when we least expect it—perhaps in a story we tell or a phrase—and not necessarily when we are directly communicating our point. Kim shows how indirect communication honors the listener's subjectivity and allows for a spiritual connection to take place. The sermon seemingly "meanders," but not in an aimless way, moving closer and closer to the desired intention.

A way of getting at indirection is through the form of letter writing. Reading Martin Luther King Jr.'s "Letter from Birmingham Jail," we can feel removed from the white pastors King addresses, and yet perhaps "overhear" the message. Preacher and homiletics professor Teresa Fry Brown has preached a "Letter from Jarena Lee," in which Lee describes the struggles of black women to follow the call of God in their lives.[4] Listeners to this sermon may not feel that Jarena Lee is speaking to them, but by indirection and overhearing, they may learn more about the experiences of black women and the oppression women have faced in following a call to preach.

Frank A. Thomas, author of *How to Preach a Dangerous Sermon,* has given preachers a road map, a kind of form, for developing a sermon that awakens the moral imagination of the hearers. Thomas describes four components of moral imagination through posing questions that help us create an experience for our listeners. You can envision four components serving as a layered form—not necessarily separate sections, but overlapping features that collectively serve to create an experience for the listener. Each of the questions he poses could be taken and more fully developed with a deep imagination to help expand the moral imaginations of our congregations. Two such questions are, "Where in this text do we find equality envisioned and represented by physical presence?" and, "Where in this text do we notice empathy as a catalyst or bridge to create opportunities to overcome the past and make new decisions for peace and justice?"[5] Frank Thomas' book helps preachers expand their own moral imagination, considering specific angles of entry into the text and how the sermon can call listeners to a greater moral imagination.

Another helpful resource comes from Woosung Calvin Choi, who described a "positive marginality" as a framework for preaching in multiethnic congregations, naming the different cultures present within the congregation as positive.[6] Choi summarizes five principles of a "positive marginality" in alliterative language: embrace, engage, establish, embody, and exhibit. To use Choi's positive marginality framework for writing a sermon, the first three components are especially helpful: *embrace* ethnic diversity by acknowledging and celebrating the differences present in the congregation, *engage* different perspectives by giving voice to the experiences of different groups, and *establish* cross-cultural interactions through which sharing in community can take place. As the preacher, do you know what persons of color in your congregation have experienced? If there are members of different immigrant communities, their perspectives on race and racism may be quite different from persons who have grown up in the United States. Facilitating conversations among persons from different cultural backgrounds can also be a way of celebrating the "positive marginality" that each person brings to the community of faith.

Another good book with suggestions for sermon forms that could address racism is *Prophetic Preaching: A Pastoral Approach,* by Leonora Tubbs Tisdale.[7] Some of the suggestions she provides are: an invitation to dialogue; sharing the narrative of "my story," "the biblical story," and "our story"; a letter form; an invitation to lament; and a confessional "Here I Stand" form (or, "This is what I believe"). In several of these forms, there is the opportunity to allow for an indirect movement toward the subject of racism. In others, such as an invitation to lament, the discussion of racism would be much more direct. The various crises that regularly emerge regarding race may indeed call for sermons that simply invite us to lament. Other sermons may need to invite us to dialogue. Still others may use another approach that Tisdale describes: an action structure. This form points to scriptural models for action, identifies the current areas needing our action, and then calls the listeners to act.

Beyond the Pulpit: Local Awareness and Engagement

As you work with your congregation in recognizing racism, how race continues to impact us, and responding with a call to gratitude, the conversations proceeding from your preaching can lead to discussions about what action your congregation is going to take as a result. Each congregation is different and has different gifts and contextual factors to consider. You will want to listen to the stories of your congregation and of the surrounding area to discern together what right action might look like.

Pastor and anti-racist trainer Joseph Barndt writes about the stages that can help involved congregations wanting to develop an anti-racist identity.[8] The first stage represents the earliest history of segregation in Christian churches in America, in which congregations were intentionally segregated. The intentionality of such segregation may still be within recent memory for some in a church, depending on its geographic location and history. The second stage Barndt describes as a "Club" church, in which the congregation views itself as a social club, not intentionally segregating itself, but not intentionally reaching out across difference either. The third stage he identifies as a multicultural church. While this is a good start, the multicultural church still expects persons from minority races or ethnicities to assimilate into the dominant culture of the congregation. The next three stages demonstrate an active commitment to anti-racism. Stage four involves an identity change for the congregation—beginning to see itself as an anti-racist church. Stage five involves structural changes that address the power imbalances at work within the congregation, ensuring that persons from groups previously excluded from leadership actually share in leadership positions. The sixth stage represents the changing church in a changing society, with the church actively seeking to make a difference in society toward ending racism.[9]

Barndt also identifies signs of transformation, certain actions that show change is taking place in your congregation.[10] Remembering the past and overcoming selective amnesia, intentionally repenting with a commitment to making a change, repairing damage done by seeking healing among all groups involved, and seeking reunification by building relationships with other churches are all signs that transformation is taking place. Depending on your context, there are a variety of ways your congregation can move toward these signs of transformation.

Think Locally: Studying Your Neighborhood and Its History

Remembering the past is often the easiest first step, though it still requires that we strengthen our capacity for discomfort. Recalling a history that is more painful or less noble than one's previous sense of history can be disorienting. And yet, it is a crucial component to understanding the ongoing impact of racism. Sometimes, this remembering can be facilitated through local tours and site visits.

A pastor of a multiethnic congregation, Soong-Chan Rah has written about journeys that members of his congregation have taken to sites of historic oppression. In his book *Many Colors: Cultural Intelligence for a Changing Church*, he talks about bus rides that he has been part of and helped to organize at his seminary and for congregations that travel to parts of the South, that explore the locations of the Japanese internment camps, and that provide opportunities for riders to listen to the stories of those who lived through experiences of discrimination. Members of your faith community do not need to travel far to better understand the historic legacy of racism; wherever their geographic location, there are sites nearby that can help shed light on this history.

Key to this, however, is knowing *who* is telling the story. One of my students traveled to one of the historic mission sites outside of San Antonio and brought back the brochure available to visitors. The history presented in this document made invisible the suffering of the Native Americans who were "Christianized" and "civilized" in the mission, presenting a much more positive and benevolent perspective regarding Spanish colonization.

What is the history of your congregation? Who has told its "official" story? Are there alternative versions to this history that need to be heard? Perhaps uncovered? Our histories should include both our mistakes along the way as well as the steps we have taken to change and live differently. This kind of work requires careful attention to the social history of place: Who has lived in the area surrounding your church, and how have different groups been treated by the members? If there are original documents of the faith community's founding or sermons that are available from its early leaders, you could perhaps learn something about the attitudes of members and leaders regarding "outsiders." How has the neighborhood around your congregation changed over time? How has the faith community responded to those changes? What does the demographic make-up of the surrounding area look like now?

Outreach: Creating Relationships of Mutuality

Another sign of transformation is that your congregation is making an active effort at reaching outside itself to build relationships with persons and groups previously seen as "outsiders." It is important for churches to identify how past actions have alienated persons from the community or have actively excluded them. After becoming aware of the need for repentance and a hunger for authentic community, your faith community may want to cultivate relationships with other congregations of color. One way to do this is by way of "Fearless Dialogues," an approach developed by pastoral theologian and Emory professor Gregory C. Ellison II. In the events he has hosted, Ellison brings together members of the community who come from diverse positions of power and authority, inviting them to have "hard, heart-felt conversations."[11]

But a word of caution: Soong-Chan Rah highlights the dangers of some forms of outreach in which the congregation sees itself as paternalistic benefactor for another community or individual persons. He gives the example of a workshop in which members of a predominantly white congregation were coming to learn about how they could help local immigrants who were moving into their community. Rah describes the speaker saying these words: "It's not about a handout, but a hand up."[12] He highlights the problematic sentiment in this comment, with *both* options conveying a paternalistic attitude:

> Our participation in the mission of God is not actually about either a handout or a hand up. "Handout" implies that one person has more than the other and therefore the one with everything is giving to the one who has nothing. Sometimes, there may even be the implication that the one who has nothing doesn't deserve this handout... But a "hand up" implies that one party is trying to lift up another from a bad place to a good place. Often, that means taking someone out of their cultural milieu and social context to bring them to a better place—my place.[13]

In thinking about outreach with other groups in your community, it is important to avoid both "handout" thinking *and* "hand up" thinking. All of us are equally in need of God's grace, and we are all called together to live as people of faith. Key to developing relationships with persons and communities outside your congregation is to consider the mutual interdependence of all of God's people: we all need each other, and we all need God. Let that radical equality guide your efforts at outreach.

Remember the Centrality of Gratitude

Finally, it is important to return to gratitude as an overall motivation for the work you and your congregation set out to do. We cannot motivate ourselves or our congregations through moralizing or shaming one another. Pursuing justice itself is not always motivating, either. With racism, there is often a "rationality" that points to the preservation of one's own benefits, privileges, and interests. This is why laws are also an important factor in the work for social justice. People will not always want to be involved just for the sake of justice; if they are required to act justly by the law, then they will learn to act differently or face the consequences. Legislative action is often necessary to stop current practices that harm communities of color. Your church may want to become active in calling your legislators.

But while changing laws is necessary, it has not always translated into changing hearts. Persons who are on the opposite side of a political issue may resent a law being passed and do what they can to work around the law. Your congregation needs to also work on engaging in relationships with other white people in order to help change the hearts and minds of "racism skeptics," as David Campt has called them.[14]

I have found that powerful motivation comes from gratitude, a deep awareness of all we have to be thankful for, a sense of our human need for connection, and the blessings that relationships with others can bring. Most of all, we are moved by our love for God, and the gratitude we feel for

God's loving presence in our lives—inviting us into the work of redemption and healing the wounds of our community of faith. While preaching about racism will not end racism, we can each do our part in the work, and enable the people we love and care for in our communities of faith to do the work as well. Together, in gratitude, let us participate in God's holy work.

Appendix

Preaching about Racism in Context— Sample Sermons

"DO NOT BE AFRAID"   Matthew 28:1–10

Preached at Austin Presbyterian Theological Seminary

March 31, 2018

We've heard the story, how early in the morning, so early it was not yet dawn, two Marys ventured together to go to the tomb. They went, late in the night after the Sabbath, and traveled to where Jesus had been buried. Now the text tells us a major seismic shift in the earth happened. An earthquake. Something significant was happening to the material world. And after this night, the world would never be the same.

And to mark this change, an angel appears, bright as lightning, white as snow, sitting on top of the stone that had previously entombed the lifeless body of Jesus, sealing it off from the world.

And for fear of the angel, the guards at the tomb start shaking—a shaking like the shaking of the earth—but these guards are shaking like dead men. In fear the ones who were guarding Jesus' tomb, guarding the body of a dead man, became themselves like the dead.

They shook like dead men. That's what really caught my eye when reading this text this past week. They shook like dead men, for fear of the angel. The guards, the ones presumably with swords, with the weapons. *They* were *afraid.* What were they afraid of? Yes, there is an angel, but in all the other angelic appearances in Matthew's gospel, no other person responds by becoming like the dead.

Maybe these are the same guards who watched Jesus die on the cross. The same ones who heard the centurion exclaim: "surely this was the Son of God!" The same ones present the first time there was an earthquake—when Jesus breathed his last and the curtain was torn in two. After seeing Jesus die on the cross, and spending time guarding his dead body, and now seeing an angel appear who rolls away the stone, these men had every reason to be afraid! God shakes the ground, and now these men shake with fear. Because the one who died at the hands of a violent system, God had raised from the dead.

I've been reading the book *Thursday Night Lights,* by historian Michael Hurd, a book about Texas high school football.[1] It is the story of *black* high school football in Texas. You see, for nearly 60 years, from soon after the UIL or University Interscholastic League, was created, only "any public white school" could join and compete.[2] This meant that black high school students in the state of Texas could not compete with students from the white high schools. So the black high schools had their own football teams, and they would play each other, and they were awesome, playing teams from other black high schools in the very same stadiums that the white teams in town would use the following night. Friday nights were for white football. Black high schools played their games Thursdays, or in some towns Wednesday or Tuesday, some on Saturdays.

What I'm learning in this book is not only the history of football at black high schools but also the history of education in Texas for African Americans. White Texans resisted educating African Americans after emancipation, and when black schools finally began to be included in public education in the 1920s and '30s, black teachers and black schools were given a fraction of the funding sent to white schools.[3] And this segregation between black schools and white schools, just as in other parts of the South, was maintained through the threat of violence, or actual violent acts.

In the small town of Conroe, which is north of Houston, north of The Woodlands, in 1920, a black man named Joe Winters had been secretly having an affair with a white woman. He was hunted down by a mob and chained to a stake in front of the town courthouse. There he was killed in front of the town square, doused with oil and kerosene and set aflame while white men as well as white women and children had gathered to watch.[4] I think of that man, Joe Winters, and I think: "what if God had raised *him* from the dead?" Just how scared would those lynchers be at the sight of his empty tomb?!

Also in Hurd's book, he writes of how segregation was enforced not only with blacks but also with whites who refused to accept the terms of white supremacy, who tried to educate black students. Hurd writes of two white Northerners who had made it down to Texas in 1870 to teach members of the recently freed black population, but who ended up dead. Two white men from Illinois had come down to teach freedmen in a school for blacks in East Texas. One mysteriously disappeared. A second was later found drowned in the river. It was said that he fell, but it was widely believed that he had been murdered because of his refusal to abide by the rules of segregation.[5]

What if today we tried going to the gravesite of these white teachers? Or to that of Viola Liuzzo, the white woman and mom of five killed by the Klan in 1965 after she helped drive civil rights protestors back and forth across Alabama, or Heather Heyer, the young white woman killed last year in Charlottesville when a white supremacist drove his car through a crowd of protestors? What if we went to these gravesites and found them empty?

What of the black and brown men and women killed by a violent system? Stephon Clark, Anthony Weber, Alton Sterling, Philando Castile, or Sandra Bland. What if went to visit their headstones, and instead of seeing tombs, we saw *them*, back in the flesh, walking around. What if God raised *these* men and women from the dead?

Imagine those responsible for these deaths, or onlookers to these deaths, and all those who have witnessed the deaths of those who have died at the hands of a violent system: what if we were suddenly witnesses to the resurrection of these very same people we have seen killed?

We too may begin to shake like dead men.

One commentary on Matthew says this about the guards: "Those who had thought they were alive now discover what they took for life is death."[6] That is the fear that grips these guards, making them shake like dead men. "What they took for life is death."

But they are not the only ones afraid: the women too, are fearful. But theirs is a different kind of fear. Their fear is coupled with great joy, becoming the first evangelists sent out to tell the others that Jesus is risen.

In many ways we have every reason to be afraid. And yet also to have joy.

We have every reason to fear, and every reason to rejoice: God knows all about it. And God has raised Christ from the dead. Christ comes to us, saying "Rejoice! Do not be afraid!" In Christ, the dead too shall rise. Those who have been murdered will also rise from the dead. Rejoice! Do not be afraid.

We rejoice that God is not done with us yet, that Christ is still shaking us up, shaking our world, calling us to challenge the powers of death that continue to crucify the oppressed and marginalized. We are afraid, because this is a great responsibility, to work for the kingdom of God, to proclaim the resurrection of the dead when so much of the structures of power depend on death and the threat of death in order to maintain control.

But in Christ we do not fear the dead. In Christ we are freed to live. In Christ we too are raised to new life, joyful and rejoicing that Christ has met us where we are, and has sent us out to go tell the others: Christ is risen. And he is going ahead of you to meet you where you are going. Yes, we go in fear, but also with great joy. Hearing Christ's words, "Do Not Be Afraid."

We are called to go out, shaking up this world, taking part in God's shake-up of the forces of death. Let us be part of this shaking. And let us not be afraid. Amen.

"WHAT ARE YOU AFRAID OF?"   Mark 16:1–8

Preached at Austin Presbyterian Theological Seminary

April 3, 2018

I preached in this pulpit just three days ago, on Saturday, for the Great Vigil of Easter. My text that evening was Matthew's account of Jesus' resurrection. This morning I'm reading from Mark. And what I noticed right away was that Matthew leaves out Salome! Here she is in Mark, the only time she is mentioned in the New Testament, in Mark's account of who was there at the foot of Jesus on the cross, and of who first went to the tomb. And then her name gets dropped from the account when Matthew takes up his pen and borrows from Mark. Why is Salome left out of Matthew's gospel?

The other, and perhaps more glaring difference, is that the supposed ending of Mark's gospel is right here, at verse 8, with the women saying nothing to anyone, for they were afraid. How can that really be the ending? Others were scandalized enough by it to ad-lib a few more sentences there at the end in later versions. They wanted to fill out the picture beyond the women's fear.

So we have a woman, Salome, who is later erased from the account, and Mark's account ending with fear. What I appreciate about Mark's gospel is its naming of Salome, and its naming of fear. The naming of Salome and the naming of fear are, for me, related.

For persons like Salome, Mary Magdalene, and Mary the mother of James, the threat of being erased, of being forgotten, of becoming invisible, was no doubt part of their oppression as women. And oppression of any kind tends to cultivate fear.

Oppression is a big word and means different things to different people, but philosopher Iris Marion Young captured it well through these five faces: exploitation, marginalization, powerlessness, cultural imperialism, and violence.[7] Exploitation can be seen in the expectation that women do particular forms of labor without getting paid: child-rearing, home management, etc. Marginalization is the dismissal of women's contributions or their relegation to supportive roles. Powerlessness can be summarized by a recent visiting scholar who said: "women can be either likable or capable, but not both." In other words, women may feel powerless in the face of cultural expectations: to be nice and friendly, or, competent and unlikeable. Cultural imperialism: this could be seen in the expectation that a male form of professionalism—for example no emotionality, no accommodation for childcare—is the standard culture for what it means to be professional. And of course, the fifth face of oppression: violence. This needs no explanation.

Iris Marion Young's five faces of oppression help us to see the multifaceted nature of oppression. And seeing Salome's name appearing here, and elsewhere erased, reminds me of the oppression of women, and helps me put into perspective the fear they felt at leaving the tomb.

Now forgetting a woman's name may not seem like oppression to everyone. But it's not just that Salome's name was later forgotten in subsequent gospel renderings. It's that her presence was effectively erased, and even disfigured.

How many of you have the association in your mind of Salome with the daughter of Herodias? The one who supposedly danced so seductively before Herod that he offered her whatever she wanted, and, prompted by her mother, asked for the head of John the Baptist? Anyone associate that character with Salome? Herodias's daughter is not named in Mark and Matthew's report of John's beheading.

But later writers—Josephus, the first-century historian and Oscar Wilde, a 19th-century playwright—name the daughter of Herodias as Salome, and so her image has become that of a seductive dancing murderer of John the Baptist.

Trying to research the name "Salome" demonstrated the ambiguity: on Wikipedia: there's an entry for Salome the disciple, Salome the play, Salome the daughter of Herodias, as well as more recent examples of women named Salome. One, a Dominican poet from the 19th century caught my eye.

Salomé Ureña was a Dominican poet and also a champion of women's education. She established the first higher education center for girls in the Dominican Republic in 1881. She was of mixed race, with African lineage, but here is the interesting thing about her name and image as it has been recorded: a scholar who compared her daguerreotype (the original photography) to the statues currently on display, noticed how any sign of her blackness has been erased. She is presented as phenotypically white, and the author says that this erasure of her blackness took place in an era of anti-blackness, and that her canonization as a celebrated Dominican poet has also coincided with a solidification of her image as a maternal figure, a respectable woman,[8] focusing on these traditional traits rather than her radical efforts to educate women.

So one Salome, whose name is later dropped from the resurrection accounts and is generally associated with beheading John the Baptist, and another Salome, whose blackness is dropped from her visual representations and hailed as traditional, both share in a disfiguring of their identity. A loss of control over their identity.

Ten days ago, here at the seminary we hosted an Oral History Project directed by our alum Steve Miller. As a faculty advisor to the project, I was given the privilege of conducting a few of the interviews. One of them was a woman who left her country in Central America to follow her husband for a job in the United States. She had a successful career in her home country, but felt the opportunity for her husband was too great to miss, so she agreed to the move. She spoke of how hard the transition was. From speaking in Spanish to having to speak and even think in English. From being a professional to having no recognizable credentials that she could use to work in the United States. From being among the elite in society to being considered, well, an outsider. She said that as soon as she opens her mouth, and people hear her Spanish accent, all the stereotypes and associations people have of Spanish-speaking persons are put on her: they assume she is an illegal immigrant, or that she crossed the border; they assume she is from Mexico (which to her was strange, since where she is from, they viewed Mexicans as aristocratic snobs). People hear her accent and assume that she is unskilled, that she cannot understand English, that she does not belong here. Her past is erased. All her status, all her accomplishments, all gone.

And so if that is how women have been treated for two millennia— their names forgotten, their reputations morphing into hyperboles of vice or virtue, then no wonder the women left the tomb scared.

They knew that whatever they said, they would not be believed. Even in the added version of Mark's ending, where someone has added additional verses—even there, the women are not believed. Their testimony is not received as valid. Their experience not trusted. Their embodied encounter at the empty tomb—all in their heads.

So I'd like to go to verse 8, where Mark writes: "they went out and fled from the tomb, for terror and amazement had seized them; and they said nothing to anyone, for they were afraid."

And ask: What if that was the end of the story? What if they truly had said nothing to anyone, out of their fear? Out of their experiences of being disbelieved and mistrusted? What if the entrenched oppression that hemmed them in, the daily reminders that their perspective didn't matter, what if all that kept them trapped in silence? Then the rest of the world would've been kept in the dark. The story wouldn't have been written. Jesus would still be waiting for the world to hear the good news that he is risen!

If the women had let their fear entomb their good news, none of us would be *here*, in this chapel, in a seminary, preparing for Christian ministry. The trajectory of the gospel going out to all the world depends upon the testimony of these three women!

Somehow, they refused to allow their fear to get in their way.

What are you afraid of? What are the messages you have been told over and over again that at times silence you?

Depending on aspects of your identity, maybe your fear comes from the history of racism in this country. People of color stopped by the police fear for their physical safety, fearing for their own lives.

As ICE agents continue to harass persons they suspect of being illegal immigrants, persons without documents fear being separated from their loved ones, afraid to even leave the house or go to school.

Women walking to their cars at night, or stepping into a taxi or Uber, fear for their physical safety. Through the #MeToo movement, women are reminded that they are not alone in the abuse they've suffered, and that the problem of sexual harassment is still pervasive.

These are fearful times. For those of you about to graduate, some of you are asking: "what's next for me?" perhaps feeling sent out from Jesus' empty tomb with nowhere to go.

What are *you* afraid of?

What have been the aspects of your identity that have made you feel physically targeted, silenced, or stripped of your dignity altogether?

For Salome as well as Mary Magdalene and Mary the mother of James, the good news of that first Easter morning was that Christ recognized them as capable evangelists. Christ recognized who they were, allowing them to be the first to witness the empty tomb.

And Christ's resurrection did something more than affirm them as worthy preachers, though that is significant—still today, the majority of Christians around the world worship in congregations that do not ordain women as preachers. We are still forgetting Christ's first choice of preachers!

But more than a message to those who deny women's call to preach, Christ's resurrection was a message to the women themselves, as well as to all who are oppressed: that even when what we fear the most actually happens, when we are forgotten, when we are abandoned, when our identities are maligned or taken from us, when we are rejected, when we are stripped of our dignity, when we die: when what we fear the most actually happens, God still has the final word. God always has the final word.

These women saw Christ humiliated, stripped of his status as a rabbi and teacher, forgotten and rejected by his disciples, and they witnessed his body abused and his terrible death. He experienced what oppressed peoples face. And yet. And yet! God raised this very Jesus from the dead, elevating him as the Son of God, giving him the highest status there is, sitting at the right hand of God, remembered and praised through all the world, alive again and for all eternity. God took into Godself the experiences of the oppressed, and turned them inside out.

So I want to say to the women fleeing from the empty tomb and to all of us here today: God sees your fear. God knows what you have faced and experienced. And in Christ, God has not forgotten you! In Christ, God has declared your identity to be a child of God! In Christ, every fear we have is crushed with the weight of that heavy stone, rolled away from the tomb, opening the way for you and me to follow where God leads. Amen.

"WADE IN THE WATER"   Sermon on Acts 8:26–40

Preached at University United Methodist Church, Austin, Texas

April 29, 2018

The book of Acts is full of amazing stories, as the early apostles went about spreading the news about Jesus Christ. Our text this morning is one such story, and I want to set it in a larger context. The reason Philip is going far away from Jerusalem, is that the church is being persecuted. This is just after the stoning of Stephen. Stephen is proclaiming the history of the faith, telling the story of God's people from their beginning to the present, and he makes his listeners enraged. Before the crowd goes in to stone him, they lay their coats at the feet of one named Saul, whom we will later come to know as Paul, who, it was written, "approved of killing" Stephen.

So our story this morning, I want to put it in context. There has just been a mob attack on a man named Stephen. He was stoned to death. In our Bible, we have recorded a lynching. And one of the people in that mob, who stood by and approved of it all, was Saul, who later becomes Paul, the author of a lot of the writings in our New Testament.

Just this past week, in Montgomery, Alabama, a new museum opened for the first time. Called the National Memorial for Peace and Justice, it is essentially a memorial to those men and women who were lynched by mobs, accompanied by plenty of people like Saul, who approved of the killing. The *Montgomery Advertiser* on Thursday on its front page presented 313 names of lynching victims and highlighted its own role in carelessly covering these deaths, assuming the victims were guilty of crimes, admitting it was "careless in how it covered mob violence and the terror foisted upon African-Americans from Reconstruction through the 1950s."

So the context for our reading this morning reminds us of the history of lynching, even in the earliest days of the church, where people of faith were often there at the sidelines, approving of the killing.

Following Stephen's murder-by-mob, a "severe persecution began" (Acts 8:1). Philip takes off and goes to Samaria, where he begins to convert whole groups of people. Then he hears the Holy Spirit telling him to go to the road from Jerusalem to Gaza, known as the wilderness road, which is where our story picks up today.

And here Philip comes across a man in a chariot. A man who is called the Ethiopian eunuch. He is an official in the court of Queen Candace of Ethiopia, in charge of all her treasury.

Now it says the Ethiopian eunuch had been up to Jerusalem to worship. But he may not have even been allowed to enter the temple. As a eunuch, he would have been prevented from participating. He is marked as an outsider. He would have had to remain outside the temple, outside the group known by circumcision. And he is from far, far away. The wilderness road suggests a sense that this is well outside the city.

The Ethiopian here stands in for all sorts of difference, and even though he is converted and baptized through his encounter with Philip, his status as an outsider still remains. He is an Ethiopian, which for persons in the Roman empire, meant the end of the world.[9] He is from far away.

As an outsider, a foreigner, a person marked as a eunuch, he had several markers of difference. As an Ethiopian, he would have had a darker skin tone than Philip. Ancient Greek and Roman artistic representations show persons from Ethiopia: they were black.

Early biblical scholars framed this story as one of difference, showing the gospel overcoming a broad distance. But they have marked as insignificant his ethnicity. Biblical scholar Clarice Martin has highlighted this omission, pointing out that by looking at the Ethiopian eunuch's outsider status and ignoring his blackness, we are missing out on where God may be at work in this text.[10]

In 1903 W.E.B. DuBois wrote a book called *The Souls of Black Folk*. He wrote that the problem of the 20th century was the problem of the color line. In 2018 the color line is still a problem.

But how we frame this problem makes all the difference!

DuBois pointed out that often the problem is inscribed onto black bodies themselves: while never asked directly, DuBois said that he was regularly approached with the sentiment: "How does it feel to be a problem?"

By marking the Ethiopian with difference, we make him the problem. We make his difference, his otherness, into a problem. We make his blackness a problem.

How do we still ask that question today? Often I hear white people telling me that they feel people of color should be the ones to talk about racism. They feel uncomfortable bringing it up because they are white. But if we wait for people of color to be the ones to bring up racism, we are essentially saying: this is your problem. Not mine.

James Cone, the father of Black Liberation Theology, died yesterday. He was known for his provocative work, extending four decades, in which he declared that God is black. Christ is black: "The blackness of Christ clarifies the definition of him as the Incarnate One…By becoming a black person, God discloses that blackness is not what the world says it is. Blackness is a manifestation of the being of God in that it reveals that neither divinity nor humanity reside in white definitions but in liberation from captivity."[11]

So let us return to our text this morning, with this view of blackness disclosing who God is, showing us that white definitions of humanity and divinity fail to accurately represent who God is and who we are.

As we return to this story, the story of the Ethiopian eunuch, I want us to do three things. The first is to reject a paternalistic reading of the text. By that I mean, recognize how past readings of this text may reinforce a pattern of seeing others as a "problem." So the first thing we do is to reject a reading of this text that makes the Ethiopian into a problem to be solved or someone in need of help. Instead of seeing him as an outsider and someone in need of saving, let us notice what gifts and insight he had. He was the official over the treasury of Queen Candace of Ethiopia. This shows a long history of civilization in Ethiopia—long before white Europeans tried to justify the slave trade by arguing that persons needed to be Christianized, and that enslaving them would bring them to God. They didn't need anyone to bring them to God! They were already Christian! Starting here, with the Ethiopian eunuch!

So the first thing is to avoid a paternalistic reading of the text. The second thing I want us to do as we read this text is to look for ways it can shed light on our current situation. Using our imagination, I think we can draw connections between this text and other issues present in our society today.

For instance, I invite you to imagine with me this story of Philip and the Ethiopian eunuch in a contemporary setting. Picture the wilderness road as a paved road outside of town. Philip is sent to this particular spot, where he sees a man in a carriage, or a car. It's a fancy car. New, shiny, nice.

But this man has been pulled over by the police. The lights are on, the cop is shining bright flood lamps through the back of the vehicle. The officer gets out of the cop car with his hand on his hip, close to his gun, and approaches the window. Philip can overhear their conversation.

"Is this your vehicle?" The Ethiopian eunuch says: "Yes sir." "It's a very fancy car you're driving. Are you sure it's not stolen?" "Yes sir. I'm the CEO of the Treasury for Queen Candace. This is my car, sir." The officer asks him to get out of the car, ordering him to put his hands against the car, while the cop pats him down, checking his pockets and pant legs for any hidden weapons. The Ethiopian eunuch looks over at Philip. Philip can see tears of fear and embarrassment in his eyes. They both have seen the news. They both know how this can turn out: very, very badly. Philip's heart is beating fast as he walks up slowly, asking the officer if there is a problem. The cop sees him, and tells the Ethiopian eunuch he can get back in his car, and he writes him a ticket for changing lanes without a signal.

Philip comes up to him and says: "Hey, man. I saw what just happened. I'm really sorry. Are you OK?" And out of the Ethiopian's mouth come these words: "Like a sheep he was led to the slaughter, and like a lamb silent before its shearer, so he does not open his mouth. In his humiliation justice was denied him. Who can describe his generation? For his life is taken away from the earth."

In Jesus Christ, and in scripture, we see the experience of the oppressed. These texts are not ancient stories, but mirrors into today. They call our attention to the presence of God in the midst of suffering, in the midst of humiliation, and they invite us to wade into the waters.

I said I wanted us to do three things with this text this morning. The first was to reject a reading of the text that presented the Ethiopian eunuch as a problem or perpetual outsider in need of saving. The second was to imagine how this text can illuminate our current situation. The third is to enter the story ourselves.

Let's take a walk. Let us together enter into this story ourselves. Not as Philip, but as a witness. We are walking beside a body of water. Fog is rising up from the water, and you see two people. One is in a chariot, the other on foot. You see the scene play out again before you: Philip comes alongside the chariot, listening to the man's voice from inside, and then receives an invitation to enter the chariot and sit beside him. You see Philip get in the chariot. Two men, sitting together, from different parts of the world. Sitting beside each other like friends, equals. Having a conversation. Learning about one another. And then the chariot stops, and the men get out, and now, you don't know what is happening, but they are going into the water. They go down into the water together, the water drenching their skin and clothes up to their heads. They both rise together, brown and black faces shining in the sun. They turn to face you, and they invite you to join them. Entering the story ourselves, we experience the bonding of two people, the building of a relationship, the dual-baptism that happens in this moment. You see, in the Greek, it says "he baptized him," but the names are not specified. What if Philip was being baptized also by the Ethiopian? What if together they were each baptized into a new relationship with one another? Into a new reality of God's in-breaking reign?

And what if, in the midst of the stories of pain we hear about, from the history of lynching and ongoing experiences of police brutality to the legacy of racism in our society today, what if all of us were invited to wade into these waters as well? Waters where we are all baptized into Christ's death and resurrection, raised to new life, invited into relationship with one another in new ways. Here is water—what is to prevent us from being baptized? Amen.

"GOLIATHS"   1 Samuel 17:1a, 4–11, 19–23, 32–49

Preached at University Presbyterian Church, San Antonio, Texas

June 23, 2018

We all love a good story, don't we? There is something so epic about David and Goliath—it's one of the stories that we tend to teach to children—we omit some of the bloodier battles and other more mature elements of the Old Testament narrative, but we teach our children about David and Goliath.

The story has this timeless quality to it, the small underdog defeating the giant, a story that connects to the feeling humanity often shares: of being small, of being unarmed, left unprotected with no armor that can fit us. And yet... and yet...there are moments when even the underdog wins. When even the Davids of the world beat the Goliaths, when even we, in our smallness, are able to accomplish something great, and overcome great obstacles.

It's an encouraging message. A hopeful tale. We can see why so many artists throughout history have chosen to depict it. Michelangelo's statue of David, perhaps one of the more famous images of David, stands in the Accademia Gallery of Florence, Italy, at almost 17 feet tall, made entirely of marble. I got to see it in person during a college trip nearly 20 years ago, and I still remember the feeling it gave me. Having seen the images of Michelangelo's David, I could recognize it immediately, but being in its presence, I found it to be something altogether marvelous. The size, the contours, the lifelikeness, the very image of a handsome, 17-foot-tall young man. And looking at his face, this rock hard stare looking out at an imagined Goliath, you see in this face the whole story—slight wrinkles around the eyes and muscles in the forehead that suggest a look of fear, but it is also a face set with determination, a steely bravery, muscles taught but relaxed, preparing to inflict the fatal blow, the essence of a king-in-the-making, the man after God's own heart.

We love David. We love his rise from nothing—the last of eight sons, a shepherd—to becoming the chosen one of God, a musician for king Saul, and eventually, king himself. And even his faults, the story of David taking Bathsheba for his wife and killing Uriah the Hittite, even these faults make him somehow more relatable—an imperfect ruler who repents when he realizes he has done wrong. And so, knowing the whole story, we are already rooting for David. We know he will be victorious. And it makes a great story. Killing a giant with a single stone from a sling.

But I also have some reservations about this story. I wonder—how does this story function in the larger narrative of the nation-state? As a story of a battle between one man and a formidable warrior, the story of David and Goliath becomes an emblem of the battle between the Israelites and the Philistines. The Philistines have routed the Israelites. Many are fearful and have hidden themselves in caves. And so Goliath represents this scary opponent. In one man, we have projected all the fears of a whole nation. And David, against all odds, defeats him by slinging a rock to the one place of vulnerability through all Goliath's armor—his forehead. And from there the Israelites rise to battle and rout the enemy, sending them running in every direction. It's a story about the turning point in a battle, when things looked their worst for the home team, and then the winds change, and your side begins to win.

But let's take a step back. Who were these Philistines? They were a neighboring tribe. They shared a border. They did commerce together. The Philistines did the blacksmithing work, forging the Israelites' ploughshares, axes, and sickles—the tools they needed to farm the land (1 Sam. 13:19-20). And they fought a lot of battles. In some the Philistines won and killed many of the Israelites (1 Sam. 4:10), and in others the Israelites won and killed many Philistines (1 Sam. 7:10-11). The territory of the two warring tribes was constantly being fought and contested.

And in the midst of these many stories of battle in the book of Samuel, you have this tale of David defeating Goliath, where Goliath is the very image of the scary Philistines, who are frightening and strong, and yet, who the Israelites were able to defeat with God's help.

Do you see what is happening here? The contested borders of two groups, battles justified through an appeal to God's will—this is the kind of story we see repeated in our own history, where one battle is used to stand in for a larger fight between two groups.

It made me think of the Alamo. Having grown up in San Antonio, remembering the Alamo was never difficult. We took Texas history in fourth and seventh grade, and studied the story of the sacrifice of the men who defended the Alamo—a mission site—and who lost their lives to the deadly Santa Ana. This story of defeat presented the Texans as an underdog group of pioneers just trying to fight for the right to be free. Their dying at the Alamo became a way of vilifying Mexico—look at how terrible Santa Ana was. It was a terrible defeat for Texans, so fighting against Mexico for their independence was only natural, and even God-ordained. At least, so the story goes.

Having lived in other parts of the country before returning to live in Austin, I came back to Texas with some skepticism. Is that all there is to the story? Randolph Campbell, author of *The Empire for Slavery: The Peculiar Institution in Texas*, helped me learn some of the background that goes unsaid in the way we teach Texas history.[12] You see, we don't teach anything about slavery when we teach about Texas history. It was true when I was growing up, and anecdotally from my son's experience, it's still true. My son who is 11 learned Texas history in the fourth grade and said he did not hear a thing about slavery until the following year, learning U.S. history. So somehow we neglect to educate about the existence of slavery in the forming of Texas.

Campbell points out that Spain, which originally controlled the area where Moses Austin and his son Stephen came to request land for a colony, permitted slavery. But a few short years after the Austins came to settle, Mexico gained its independence from Spain. And Mexico outlawed slavery, freeing all the slaves in what was now Mexico. Now, for Stephen F. Austin this created a problem, since the early colony needed more settlers to join them. He would not be able to convince wealthy, slave-owning white Southerners to move to Texas if they had to free their slaves at the border. There is documentation of Stephen F. Austin declaring to the Mexican government in his letters of appeal that "Texas must be a slave country."[13] So fighting for independence from Mexico was also about fighting for the ability to keep some men and women perpetually un-free, in bondage, as slaves. But that does not fit neatly into our story about the Alamo and sacrifice.

I share this side of Texas history to highlight that the way we tell our history—the way we tell our battle stories—involves a lot of Goliaths that we create. In the Battle of the Alamo, our Goliath was this mean and scary Santa Ana, a formidable dictator, who needed to be defeated, and Texans winning their independence at the Battle of San Jacinto meant the "good guys" won...right?

We keep creating our Goliaths, painting the big and scary opponents we face as these monsters, which makes it easier for us to call forth our bravery and determination to defeat our enemies. But who are these Goliaths, really?

On the campaign trail of 2016, in order to argue for a border wall, then-candidate Trump called persons from Mexico gang members, drug dealers, and rapists. Calling for a border wall was a way of saying, I will stop these scary people from crossing into our territory! I will defeat them! I will bring down Goliath!

And then last week, we heard that being strong on immigration meant defending this country against being "overrun." Another Goliath—a big scary fear of immigrants taking over this country. A scary Goliath who takes away jobs and depletes national resources. Throughout our history as a nation, we have constantly turned immigrants into monsters: Poles, Czechs, Jews, Italians, the Chinese, the Japanese, groups we have personified as our Goliaths, telling ourselves stories of why we should fear them, inciting mistrust and fear to keep them out. Who will slay this Goliath? And of course, Europeans were the first immigrants to overrun this country, battling Native Americans and claiming territory for ourselves. Surely we were the Goliaths who kept on advancing. But it is hard for us to see ourselves as Goliath. We would rather side with the underdog. Because it is so easy to feel small in the world, to feel like a child. It is easy to forget the power we possess.

Despite efforts to paint a picture of immigrants as Goliaths, we have seen very different images over the past several weeks. We've seen small children separated from their families. Kids taken away from their parents by our government. Not drug dealers or gang members, but children. These are not giants. You can't turn these tiny humans into something we should fear. These little ones are not taking our jobs.

So instead, the real Goliath is revealed to be our own nation's leadership. At its top ranks, there is the Goliath who bears down on us and makes us feel too small.

And yet...we saw this past week, people on both sides of the political divide making statements and calls and demands that this process of separating families stop. And our Goliath-in-chief stops requiring border agents to separate families at the border. For those of us who felt like the underdog, throwing stones at a giant, seeing this turn of events may have given us some bit of good news.

You may be worried about this sermon being political. But this is a political text. This text is part of the larger narrative of a nation-state justifying its existence, its leadership, and its military tactics. And it's important that we see it as such, and with that lens, consider the stories we tell about our own nation. What are the stories we tell about our leadership? About our military tactics? Who are the Goliaths of our own making?

Earlier I described the artistic rendering of David by Michelangelo in a 17-foot-tall statue of marble. But I wanted to close with a different portrayal. I wanted to evoke for you a painting by another Italian by the name of Caravaggio, a painter who was known for his stark contrasts of dark and light in his paintings, and his sometimes-gory details. There are at least three paintings by Caravaggio of David with Goliath, and the one I want to lift up for us is the one in which he paints his own face onto the face of Goliath. In the painting, David is shown as a very young man, more like a boy, holding by the hair the decapitated head of Goliath, whose face bears the resemblance of Caravaggio's own face. And the boy David, looking out at the head, looks on not with triumph or disgust, but rather, compassion.

Why did Caravaggio paint his own face as the face of Goliath? And why the look of compassion on the face of David looking down at the head of his foe? I'm not sure. But I want to leave us with this image, an image that evokes our own role as Goliath, our face on the face of Goliath. Our own hands painting onto Goliath the faces of our enemies, those we fear. I imagine that boyish face of David in Caravaggio's painting, that face that looks with compassion on Goliath, to be the look that God has on God's face, looking down at the carnage that is our world community, seeing the ways we have torn this body apart.

God has compassion on us, and loves us, and calls us to remember Christ's body, broken for us, and yet brought back to life, declaring a resounding no to death and destruction, and yes to life. It is in the hope of God's love, fully revealed in the face of Jesus Christ, that we give all our stories up to God, and pray for God to enfold us into the larger story of God's redemption of humanity, uniting Davids with Goliaths. No longer foes, but friends. Amen.

Notes

Chapter 1:
Preaching to Ourselves: Beginning with Gratitude

[1]Paul Ricoeur, *The Course of Recognition*, trans. David Pellauer (Cambridge, Mass.: Harvard University Press, 2007).

[2]Beverly Daniel Tatum, "Talking About Race, Learning About Racism: The Application of' Racial Identity Development Theory," *Harvard Educational Review* 62, no. 1 (1992): 1.

[3]*Sin* language is harmful when we identify all forms of "pride" as sin, which allows abusers to insist their victims accept their "humble" position and status. Sinful pride is different from honoring oneself as equal to all people made in the image of God. See Serene Jones's *Feminist Theory and Christian Theology: Cartographies of Grace* (Minneapolis: Fortress Press, 2000).

[4]While I tend to avoid the language of "white privilege," for many people it is a very helpful concept for recognizing the continuing effects of racism. See Peggy McIntosh, "White Privilege: Unpacking the Invisible Knapsack," in Monica McGoldrick, ed., *Re-Visioning Family Therapy: Race, Culture, and Gender in Clinical Practice*, (New York: Guilford Press, 1998). At the same time, denouncing our privilege does not *do* anything in the sense of eliminating that privilege. See Sarah Ahmed, "Declarations of Whiteness: The Non-Performativity of Anti-Racism," available online at: http://www.borderlands.net.au/vol3no2_2004/ahmed_declarations.htm

[5]Adam C. Wright, "Teachers' Perceptions of Students' Disruptive Behavior: The Effect of Racial Congruence and Consequences for Schools Suspension." Cited by Dick Startz, "Teacher Perceptions and Race," Brookings website, Feb. 22, 2016, accessed online April 13, 2018, at https://www.brookings.edu/blog/brown-center-chalkboard/2016/02/22/teacher-perceptions-and-race/

[6]Ping Cheng, Zhenguo Lin, and Yingchun Liu, "Racial Discrepancy in Mortgage Rates," *Journal of Real Estate Finance and Economics* 51, 1 (July 2015), accessed online April 13, 2018, at https://www.researchgate.net/publication/264555748_Racial_Discrepancy_in_Mortgage_Interest_Rates

[7]Gene Demby, "For People of Color, a Housing Market Partially Hidden from View," *Code Switch: Race and Identity Remixed*, npr.org, June 17, 2013, accessed online October 1, 2018, at https://www.npr.org/sections/codeswitch/2013/06/17/192730233/for-people-of-color-a-housing-market-partially-hidden-from-view

[8]Vilma Ortiz and Edward Telles, "Racial Identity and Racial Treatment of Mexican Americans," *Race and Social Problems* 4.1 (2012), accessed online August 9, 2018, at https://www.ncbi.nlm.nih.gov/pmc/articles/PMC3846170/

[9]Wendy Ashley, "The Angry Black Woman: The Impact of Pejorative Stereotypes on Psychotherapy with Black Women," *Journal of Social Work in Public Health*, Vol 29:1 (2014): 27–34, available online: https://doi.org/10.1080/19371918.2011.6194 49

¹⁰View links to several studies here: https://www.cnn.com/2016/12/20/health/black-men-killed-by-police/index.html

¹¹Diana Butler Bass, *Grateful: The Transformative Power of Giving Thanks* (New York: HarperOne, 2018). While Bass's book came out after I had completed the earliest drafts of this manuscript, many ideas she presents would deepen this conversation about gratitude as a practice.

¹²I use the term "kin-dom," from the work of Ada María Isasi-Díaz, who uses kin-dom instead of kingdom to show the mutuality of relationships with God's realm. See *Mujerista Theology* (Maryknoll, N.Y.: Orbis Books), 1996.

Chapter 2: The Role of Interpretation and Recognition

¹The full transcript of our interview can be found at: http://kut.org/post/its-white-people-discuss-and-confront-racism-minister-says

²See, for example, Eduardo Bonilla-Silva, *Racism without Racists: Color-Blind Racism and the Persistence of Racial Inequality in America*, 3d ed. (Lanham, Md.: Rowman & Littlefield, 2009); Helen Ngo, *The Habits of Racism: A Phenomenology of Racism and Racialized Embodiment* (Lanham, Md: Lexington Books, 2017); Michael Omi and Howard Winant, *Racial Formation in the United States: From the 1960s to the 1990s*, 2d ed. (New York: Routledge, 1994); and Traci West. *Disruptive Christian Ethics: When Racism and Women's Lives Matter* (Louisville: Westminster John Knox Press, 2006).

³For a discussion of the use of the term Latinx instead of Hispanic, see Ed Morales, *Latinx: The New Force in American Politics and Culture*(Brooklyn: Verso, 2018).

⁴Helen Ngo, *The Habits of Racism: A Phenomenology of Racism and Racialized Embodiment* (Lanham, Md: Lexington Books, 2017), 107.

Chapter 3: Communicating What Racism Means

¹Michael O. Emerson and Christian Smith, *Divided by Faith: Evangelical Religion and the Problem of Race in America*, (New York: Oxford University Press, 2000), 120.

²Eduardo Bonilla-Silva, *Racism without Racists: Color-Blind Racism and the Persistence of Racial Inequality in America*, third ed. (Lanham, Md.: Rowman & Littlefield Publishers, Inc., 2009).

³Mark Chesler, "Contemporary Sociological Theories of Racism," in Phyllis A. Katz, ed., *Towards the Elimination of Racism* (New York: Pergamon Press, 1976); cited by Bonilla-Silva, *Racism without Racists*, 26.

⁴Michael Omi and Howard Winant, *Racial Formation in the United States: From the 1960s to the 1990s*, second ed. (New York: Routledge, 1994), 11.

⁵See, for example, David R. Roediger, *The Wages of Whiteness: Race and the Making of the American Working Class*, revised (New York, London: Verso, 1991); Noel Ignatiev, *How the Irish Became White* (New York: Routledge, 2009).

⁶Steven Salaita, *Anti-Arab Racism in the USA: Where It Comes from and What It Means for Politics* (Ann Arbor, Mich.: Pluto Press, 2006); Sarah Gualtieri, "Becoming 'White': Race, Religion and the Foundations of Syrian/Lebanese Ethnicity in the United States," *Journal of American Ethnic History* 20, no. 4 (July 1, 2001): 29–58; Salah Hassan, "Arabs, Race and the Post-September 11 National Security State," *Middle East Report* 32, no. 224 (Fall 2002).

[7]Omi and Winant, *Racial Formation in the United States*, 55, emphasis in original.

[8]*Takao Ozawa v. United States* (1922) and *United States v. Bhagat Singh Thind* (1923). See also Ian Haney López, *White by Law: The Legal Construction of Race* (New York: NYU Press, 2006).

[9]Vilma Ortiz and Edward Telles, "Racial Identity and Racial Treatment of Mexican Americans," *Race and Social Problems* 4.1 (2012), accessed online August 9, 2018, at https://www.ncbi.nlm.nih.gov/pmc/articles/PMC3846170/ .

[10]Sharon M. Lee, "Racial Classifications in the U.S. Census: 1890–1990," *Ethnic and Racial Studies* 16, no. 1 (January 1993): 75–94; Kenneth Prewitt, "Racial Classification in America: Where Do We Go from Here?," *Daedalus* 134, no. 1 (January 1, 2005): 5–17.

[11]There was discussion of returning to pre-1977 categorization of Hispanic origin as a racial category and no longer as ethnicity. See "Census Rethinks Hispanic on Questionnaire," accessed December 30, 2013, http://www.usatoday.com/story/news/nation/2013/01/03/hispanics-may-be-added-to-census-race-category/1808087/. The 2020 Census will continue to use Hispanic origin as ethnicity: see "2020 Census to Keep Racial, Ethnic Categories in 2010," https://www.npr.org/2018/01/26/580865378/census-request-suggests-no-race-ethnicity-data-changes-in-2020-experts-say

[12]Rakesh Kochhar, Richard Fry, and Paul Taylor, "Wealth Gaps Rise to Record Highs Between Whites, Blacks, Hispanics," *Pew Social & Demographic Trends*, July 26, 2011, accessed online October 1, 2018, at http://www.pewsocialtrends.org/2011/07/26/wealth-gaps-rise-to-record-highs-between-whites-blacks-hispanics/.

[13]Chesler, "Contemporary Sociological Theories of Racism."

[14]Kimberlé Crenshaw Williams,. "Mapping the Margins: Intersectionality, Identity Politics, and Violence Against Women of Color,:" in *The Public Nature of Private Violence,* ed. Martha Albertson Fineman and Rixanne Mykitiuk (New York: Routledge, 1994), 93–118. Also available online as a pdf: https://www.racialequitytools.org/resourcefiles/mapping-margins.pdf

[15]For an analysis of anti-racism and its tendency to ignore classism, see John Hartigan Jr., *Odd Tribes: Toward a Cultural Analysis of White People* (Durham N.C.: Duke University Press, 2005); Maurianne Adams, et al., *Readings for Diversity and Social Justice: An Anthology on Racism, Antisemitism, Sexism, Heterosexism, Ableism, and Classism,* first ed. (New York: Routledge, 2000). For a theological approach connecting issues of race with sexuality, see Patrick S. Cheng, *Rainbow Theology: Bridging Race, Sexuality, and Spirit* (New York: Seabury Books, 2013).

[16]Ashley W. Doane, "Rethinking Whiteness Studies," in *White Out: The Continuing Significance of Racism* (New York: Routledge, 2003), 1–18.

[17]The most recent figures for wealth disparity from Pew Research Center stated that "Black households have only 10 cents in wealth for every dollar held by white families. In 2016, the median wealth of non-Hispanic white households was $171,000. That's 10 times the wealth of black households ($17,100) – a larger gap than in 2007." http://www.pewresearch.org/fact-tank/2018/02/22/5-facts-about-blacks-in-the-u-s/ . Other resources include Melvin L. Oliver and Thomas M. Shapiro, *Black Wealth/White Wealth: A New Perspective on Racial Inequality* (New York, London: Routledge, 1997); Mark D. Hayward and Melonie Heron, "Racial Inequality in Active Life among Adult Americans," *Demography* 36, no. 1 (February 1, 1999): 77–91; Bruce Western and Becky Pettit, "Black-White Wage Inequality, Employment Rates, and Incarceration," *American Journal of Sociology* 111, no. 2 (September 1, 2005): 553–78. On the other hand, Asian Americans as a racial category have the

greatest income inequality, with wealthy Asian Americans making 10 times the income of poorer Asian Americans. See Rakesh Kochhar and Anthony Cilluffo, "Income Inequality in the U.S. Is Rising Most Rapidly Among Asians," July 12, 2018, accessed online August 9, 2018 at *http://www.pewsocialtrends.org/2018/07/12/income-inequality-in-the-u-s-is-rising-most-rapidly-among-asians/*

[18]Michael I. Norton and Samuel R. Sommers, "Whites See Racism as a Zero-Sum Game That They Are Now Losing," *Perspectives on Pscyhological Science* 6, no. 3 (May 2011): 215–18.

[19]Ibid.

[20]See the most recent anti-affirmative action case, Fisher v. University of Texas (2016).

[21]Emerson and Smith, *Divided by Faith.*

[22]Ibid., 86.

[23]Ibid., 86–87.

[24]Ibid., 89.

[25]Ibid., 76.

[26]Ibid., 110.

[27]Ibid.,116–17.

[28]Ibid., 69–70.

[29]Peggy McIntosh, "White Privilege: Unpacking the Invisible Knapsack." Simply putting her name into a search engine should bring you to her article. Her ideas have been made accessible in training documents found online, such as the following: https://www.pcc.edu/resources/illumination/documents/white-privilege-essay-mcintosh.pdf

[30]https://www.nytimes.com/2018/03/09/us/blacks-evangelical-churches.html

[31]In *The New York Times* article cited above, a white pastor claimed that there were certain ways for addressing racial inequality: "There are larger racial injustices in the country, he said, and those injustices need to be fixed—though not in ways that would enable dependence, he clarified, but rather to "give people a hand up, not a handout." This assumption of "dependence" and "handouts" as being problematic re-centers people of color as the "problem" in racial inequality, somehow being more prone to dependence than the whites who benefit from huge tax advantages for their housing and investments, many of which can be linked to the history of white racial discrimination.

[32]http://money.cnn.com/2016/09/20/news/economy/black-white-wage-gap/index.html

[33]http://www.nytimes.com/2013/06/12/business/economy/discrimination-in-housing-against-nonwhites-persists-quietly-us-study-finds.html

[34]https://www.revealnews.org/article/for-people-of-color-banks-are-shutting-the-door-to-homeownership/

[35]http://www.newsweek.com/race-schools-592637 See also https://www.brookings.edu/research/new-evidence-on-school-choice-and-racially-segregated-schools/

[36]https://www.pbs.org/newshour/education analysis-reveals-racial-disparities-school-arrests See also http://www.bbc.com/news/science-environment-40135240 and http://www.businessinsider.com/study-finds-huge-racial-disparity-in-americas-prisons-2016-6

[37]Gordon Allport, *The Nature of Prejudice* (New York: Doubleday/And cited in http://tedcantle.co.uk/wp-content/uploads/2013/03/092-Interg contact-theory-explained-Everett-J-2013.pdf

[38]Ibid.

[39]Traci West, *Disruptive Christian Ethics: When Racism and Women's Lives Matter* (Louisville: Westminster John Knox Press, 2006), 114–16.

[40]For other examples of subtle messages, see Cody Sanders and Angela Yarber, *Microaggressions in Ministry: Confronting the Hidden Violence of Everyday Church* (Louisville: Westminster John Knox Press, 2015).

[41]Martin Luther King Jr., preaching at National Cathedral in Washington, D.C., on March 31, 1968, quoted in Joseph Barndt, *Becoming the Anti-Racist Church: Journeying Toward Wholeness* (Minneapolis: Fortress Press, 2011), 1.

[42]Emerson and Smith, *Divided by Faith.*

[43]Curtiss Paul DeYoung, et al., *United by Faith: The Multiracial Congregation as an Answer to the Problem of Race* (New York: Oxford University Press, 2004). Though the authors discuss the importance of uniracial churches for racial minorities, they overwhelmingly support multiracial congregations as an answer to racism.

[44]Korie L. Edwards, *The Elusive Dream: The Power of Race in Interracial Churches* (Oxford, New York: Oxford University Press, 2008). See also critiques of the contact hypothesis in Eileen O'Brien and Kathleen Odell Korgen, "It's the Message, Not the Messenger: The Declining Significance of Black-White Contact in a 'Colorblind' Society," *Sociological Inquiry* 77, no. 3 (August 2007): 356–82, citing Allport, *The Nature of Prejudice.*

[45]CNN posed a question to black celebrities regarding the first time they knew they were black. Their stories were made available online: https://www.cnn.com/interactive/2017/02/us/first-time-i-realized-i-was-black/

[46]The Truth and Reconciliation Oral History Project has collected videos of persons sharing their experiences of discrimination: https://hbcuoralhistoryvideoproject.org/

[47]Anne Anlin Cheng, *The Melancholy of Race: Psychoanalysis, Assimilation, and Hidden Grief* (Oxford University Press, 2001).

[48]Ibid., 103.

[49]https://www.theatlantic.com/business/archive/2016/02/blacks-hispanics-mortgages/471024/?utm_source=eb See also http://www.pewresearch.org/fact-tank/2017/01/10/blacks-and-hispanics-face-extra-challenges-in-getting-home-loans/

[50]https://www.usnews.com/opinion/blogs/policy-dose/articles/2016-04-14/theres-a-huge-health-equity-gap-between-whites-and-minorities

[51]Michelle Alexander, *The New Jim Crow: Mass Incarceration in the Age of Colorblindness*, reprint (New York: New Press, 2010).

[52]See www.davidcampt.com

[53]David W. Campt, *The White Ally Toolkit Workbook,* available to download for purchase online at https://www.whiteallytoolkit.com/new-products/white-ally-toolkit-workbook

Chapter 4:
Talking about Racial Identity with White People of Faith

[1]Korie L. Edwards, *The Elusive Dream: The Power of Race in Interracial Churches* (Oxford, New York: Oxford University Press, 2008), 84–89.

[2]Ibid., 99.

[3]Ibid., 100. Emphasis mine.

[4]Michael O. Emerson and Christian Smith, *Divided by Faith: Evangelical Religion and the Problem of Race in America* (New York: Oxford University Press, 2000), 147, citing the work of Pamela Popielarz and J. Miller McPherson, "On the Edge or in Between: Niche Position, Niche Overlap, and the Duration of Voluntary Association Memberships," *American Journal of Sociology* 101 (1995): 678–721.

[5]Emerson and Smith, *Divided by Faith*, 165.

[6]Janet Helms, *Black and White Racial Identity: Theory, Research, and Practice* (New York: Greenwood Press, 1990), 19.

[7]Helms briefly cites theorists who argue persons may enter the cycle at different stages, and perhaps may go through some of the stages more than once at different points in their lives. See Helms, *Black and White Racial Identity*, 32.

[8]Ibid., 49.

[9]Ibid.

[10]Beverly Daniel Tatum, "Talking About Race, Learning About Racism: The Application of' Racial Identity Development Theory," *Harvard Educational Review* 62, no. 1 (1992): 1.

[11]Ibid., 19, emphasis mine.

[12]Ibid., 18–21.

[13]Helms, *Black and White Racial Identity*, 56. I should also note that I have shortened the name of the fifth stage, which in Helms (and Tatum, "Talking About Race") is called "Immersion/Emersion."

[14]Ibid., 55–58.

[15]For a better understanding of "microaggression," see Derald Wing Sue, et al., "Racial Microaggressions in Everyday Life: Implications for Clinical Practice," *American Psychologist* 62, no. 4 (May 2007): 271–86.

[16]Carolyn Helsel, *Anxious to Talk about It* (St. Louis: Chalice Press, 2017).

[17]L. Festinger, A Theory of Cognitive Dissonance (Stanford, CA: Stanford University Press, 1957), cited in Helms, *Black and White Racial Identity*, 59.

[18]Ibid., 58–60.

[19]Ibid., 60–61. A good resource for this is Peggy McIntosh, "White Privilege: Unpacking the Invisible Knapsack," in Monica McGoldrick, ed., *Re-Visioning Family Therapy: Race, Culture, and Gender in Clinical Practice* (New York: Guilford Press, 1998).

[20]Helms, *Black and White Racial Identity*, 61–62.

[21]A recent book that highlights the work of white anti-racist allies is Drick Boyd, *White Allies in the Struggle for Racial Justice* (Maryknoll: Orbis Books, 2015). Boyd points to other anthologies of white anti-racists that can also be helpful for white congregants looking for role models.

[22]Tatum, "Talking About Race," 16.

[23]Helms, *Black and White Racial Identity,* 62.

[24]Helms, *Black and White Racial Identity,* 65–66.

Chapter 5: Biblical Preaching about Racism

[1]This chapter will focus specifically on the Bible as sacred text, but if you are part of a tradition that uses a different sacred text from which to preach, feel free to translate what makes the most sense for your context, and contact me with any suggestions you would like to add to the discussion.

[2]Thomas G. Long, *The Witness of Preaching,* 3d ed. (Louisville: Westminster John Knox Press, 2016).

[3]Cain Hope Felder, "Race, Racism, and the Biblical Narratives," in Cain Hope Felder, ed., *Stony the Road We Trod: African American Biblical Interpretation* (Minneapolis: Fortress Press, 1991), 144.

[4]Haddon Robinson, "Convictions of Biblical Preaching," in Haddon Robinson and Craig Brian Larsoneds., *The Art and Craft of Biblical Preaching* (Grand Rapids, Mich.: Zondervan, 2005), 23–24.

[5]Renita Weems, "Reading *Her* Way through the Struggle: African American Women and the Bible," in Cain Hope Felder, ed., *Stony the Road We Trod,* 67.

[6]Ibid.

[7]Justo L. González and Pablo A. Jiménez, *Púlpito: An Introduction to Hispanic Preaching* (Nashville: Abingdon Press, 2005).

[8]González, *Púlpito,* 28.

[9]Ibid., 28–38.

[10]Jiménez, *Púlpito,* 43. He refers in this chapter to scholars such as Virgilio Elizondo, Orlando E. Costas, Justo González, Fernando Segovia, Ada Maria Isasi-Díaz, C. Gilbert Romero, and Francisco García-Treto.

[11]Ibid., 44–45.

[12]Eunjoo Mary Kim, *Preaching the Presence of God: A Homiletic from an Asian American Perspective* (Valley Forge, Pa.: Judson Press, 1999), 34–37.

[13]Ibid., 97.

[14]Cleophus LaRue, *The Heart of Black Preaching* (Louisville: Westminster John Knox Press, 1999), 10.

[15]Cleophus LaRue, "African American Preaching and the Bible," in Brian Blount, gen. ed., Cain Hope Felder, Clarice Martin, and Emerson Powery, ass. eds., *True to Our Native Land: An African American New Testament Commentary* (Minneapolis: Fortress Press, 2007), 65–66.

[16]Frank A. Thomas, *Introduction to the Practice of African American Preaching* (Nashville: Abingdon Press, 2016), 87.

[17]Vincent Wimbush, "The Bible and African Americans: An Outline of an Interpretive History," in Cain Hope Felder, ed., *Stony the Road We Trod,* 83.

[18]Ibid., 97.

[19]Vincent L. Wimbush, "'We Will Make Our Own Future Text': An Alternate Orientation to Interpretation," in Blount, gen. ed., *True to Our Native Land,* 44.

[20]Ibid.

21John Henry Hopkids, an Episcopal Bishop in Vermont, wrote *A Scriptural, Ecclesiastical, and Historical View of Slavery, from the Days of the Patriarch Abraham, to the Nineteenth Century,* published in 1864. He claims defending slavery was an original intention of the Bible: "The Bible's defense of slavery is very plain. St. Paul was inspired, and knew the will of the Lord Jesus Christ, and was only intent on obeying it. And who are we, that in our modern wisdom presume to set aside the Word of God...and invent for ourselves a 'higher law' than those holy Scriptures which are given to us...?" Cited in Willard M. Swartley, *Slavery, Sabbath, War and Women: Case Issues in Biblical Interpretation* (Scottsdale, Pa.: Herald Press, 1983).

22Mitzi J. Smith, "Slavery in the Early Church," in Blount, gen. ed., *True to Our Native Land,* 17.

23Clarice J. Martin, "The *Haustafeln* (Household Codes) in African American Biblical Interpretation: 'Free Slaves' and 'Subordinate Women,'" in Cain Hope Felder, ed., *Stony the Road We Trod,* 215.

24State v. Mann, North Carolina, 266-267, cited in Ibid.

25Martin, "The *Haustafeln,*" 215.

26For a brief description of Jarena Lee's call to ministry and preaching vocation, see Eunjoo Mary Kim, *Women Preaching: Theology and Practice Through the Ages* (Eugene, Oreg.: Wipf & Stock, 2004), 99–104. For a brief recounting of Julia Foote's call to preaching and the obstacles facing black women called to ministry, see Teresa Fry Brown, *Weary Throats and New Songs: Black Women Proclaiming God's Word* (Nashville: Abingdon, 2003), 25–36.

27John Stott, "A Definition of Biblical Preaching," in Robinson and Larson, eds., *The Art and Craft of Biblical Preaching,* 27.

28Rick Richardson, "Cross-Cultural Preaching: How to Connect in Our Multicultural Word," in Robinson and Larson, eds., *The Art and Craft of Biblical Preaching,* 172.

29William H. Willimon, *Who Lynched Willie Earle? Preaching to Confront Racism* (Nashville: Abingdon Press, 2017).

Chapter 6: Theology for Preaching about Racism

1Different faith communities have different ways of talking about sin. If you are part of another religious faith, see what part of this "sin-talk" can be helpful for your community to explain the ramifications of sin in our world. Contact me with any suggestions you have for broadening this discussion.

2Jim Wallis, *America's Original Sin: Racism, White Privilege, and the Bridge to a New America* (Grand Rapids: Brazos Press, 2016).

3Marjorie Hewitt Suchocki, *The Fall into Violence: Original Sin and Relational Theology* (New York: Continuum, 1995).

4Rita Nakashima Brock, *Journeys by Heart: A Christology of Erotic Power* (New York: Crossroad, 1988), 7.

5Ibid., 8.

6Stephen G. Ray Jr., *Do No Harm: Social Sin and Christian Responsibility* (Minneapolis: Augsburg Fortress Press, 2003).

7Ibid., 69.

[8]Reinhold Niebuhr, "Review of *An American Dilemma* by Gunnar Myrdal," *Christianity and Society* 9, no. 3 (Summer 1944): 42.

[9]Ray, *Do No Harm*, 63; quoting Gunnar Myrdal, *An American Dilemma: The Negro Problem and Modern Democracy* (New York: Harper, 1944), 929–30.

[10]Ray, Jr., *Do No Harm*, 63; citing Myrdal, *An American Dilemma*, 929–30.

[11]Delores S. Williams, *Sisters in the Wilderness: The Challenge of Womanist God-Talk* (Maryknoll, N.Y.: Orbis Books, 1993), 164.

[12]For examples, see Gustavo Gutiérrez, *A Theology of Liberation: History, Politics, and Salvation* (Maryknoll, N.Y.: Orbis Books, 1973); Chung Hyun Kyung, *Struggle to Be the Sun Again: Introducing Asian Women's Theology* (Maryknoll, N.Y.: Orbis Books, 1990); Ada Maria Isasi-Diaz, *Mujerista Theology: A Theology for the Twenty-First Century* (Maryknoll, N.Y.: Orbis Books, 1996); and David Phillips Hansen, *Native Americans, the Mainline Church, and the Quest for Interracial Justice* (St. Louis: Chalice Press, 2016).

[13]George D. Kelsey, *Racism and the Christian Understanding of Man* (New York: Scribner, 1965).

[14]Ibid., 176.

[15]Ralph Ellison, *Invisible Man* (1952; New York: Vintage International, 1995), 3.

[16]Gregory C. Ellison II, *Cut Dead, But Still Alive: Caring for African American Young Men* (Nashville: Abingdon Press, 2013).

[17]Clarice Martin, "A Chamberlain's Journey and the Challenge of Interpretation for Liberation" *Semeia* 47 (1989): 105–35.

[18]Ada María Isasi-Díaz, *En La Lucha / In the Struggle: A Hispanic Woman's Liberation Theology.* (Minneapolis: Augsburg Fortress, 1993), 188.

[19]Ibid., 189-190.

[20]James H. Cone, *Black Theology and Black Power* (New York: Seabury Press, 1969), 32. Cone died just days before I submitted this manuscript. His 40-year career in theology was a profound contribution to theological education and the training of religious leaders. He will be missed.

[21]James H. Cone, *The Cross and the Lynching Tree* (Maryknoll: Orbis, 2011), 2.

[22]Willie James Jennings, *The Christian Imagination: Theology and the Origins of Race* (New Haven, Conn.: Yale University Press, 2010), 9.

[23]Ibid.

[24]Ibid., 248.

[25]M. Shawn Copeland, *Enfleshing Freedom: Body, Race, and Being* (Minneapolis: Fortress Press, 2009), 104.

[26]J. Kameron Carter. *Race: A Theological Account* (New York: Oxford University Press, 2008),352.

[27]Ibid., 351–52, 353.

[28]"I sighed after such freedom, but was bound not by an iron imposed by anyone else but by the iron of my own choice. The enemy had a grip on my will and so made a chain for me to hold me as prisoner. The consequence of a distorted will is passion. By servitude to passion, habit is formed, and habit to which there is no resistance becomes necessity. By these links, as it were, connected one to another (hence my term a chain), a harsh bondage held me under restraint." Saint Augustine, *Confessions*, trans. Henry Chadwick (New York: Oxford University Press, 1991), book 8, chapter 5.10, 140.

[29]Michael Eric Dyson, *Tears We Cannot Stop: A Sermon to White America.* (New York: St. Martin's Press, 2017), 26.

[30]Ibid.

[31]Ibid.

[32]Kumarini Silva, *Brown Threat: Identification in the Security State,* (Minneapolis: University of Minnesota Press, 2016), 1.

[33]Copeland, *Enfleshing Freedom*, 81.

[34]Ibid., 81.

[35]Ibid., 102–103.

[36]Brock, *Journeys by Heart*, 23.

[37]Ibid.

Chapter 7: Strategies for Preaching and Beyond

[1]Carolyn B. Helsel, *Anxious to Talk About It: Helping White Christians Talk Faithfully about Racism* (St. Louis: Chalice Press, 2017), 111–13.

[2]For more on "focus and function," see Thomas G. Long, *The Witness of Preaching,* third ed. (Louisville: Westminster John Knox Press, 2016).

[3]Eunjoo Mary Kim, *Preaching the Presence of God: A Homiletic from an Asian American Perspective* (Valley Forge, Pa.: Judson Press, 1999), 12326.

[4]Teresa Fry Brown, *Weary Throats and New Songs: Black Women Proclaiming God's Word* (Nashville: Abingdon Press, 2003),46–52.

[5]Frank A. Thomas, *How to Preach a Dangerous Sermon* (Nashville: Abingdon, 2018), 86.

[6]Woosung Calvin Choi, *Preaching to Multiethnic Congregation: Positive Marginality as a Homiletical Paradigm* (New York: Peter Lang, 2015).

[7]Leonora Tubbs Tisdale, *Prophetic Preaching: A Pastoral Approach* (Louisville: Westminster John Knox Press, 2010).

[8]Joseph Barndt, *Becoming an Anti-Racist Church: Journeying Toward Wholeness* (Minneapolis: Fortress Press, 2011).

[9]Ibid. Barndt has a useful chart identifying these six stages on 148–49.

[10]Ibid., 196–98.

[11]Gregory C. Ellison II, *Fearless Dialogues: A New Movement for Justice* (Louisville: Westminster John Knox Press, 2017).

[12]Soong-Chan Rah, *Many Colors: Cultural Intelligence for a Changing Church* (Chicago: Moody Publishers, 2010), 120–22.

[13]Ibid., 121.

[14]David W. Campt, *The White Ally Toolkit Workbook,* available to download for purchase online at https://www.whiteallytoolkit.com/new-products/white-ally-toolkit-workbook

Appendix
Preaching about Racism in Context—Sample Sermons

[1]Michael Hurd, *Thursday Night Lights: The Story of Black High School Football in Texas* (Austin: University of Texas Press, 2017).

[2]Ibid., 24 and 32.

[3]Ibid., 25 and 28.

[4]Ibid., 15.

[5]Ibid., 19-20.

[6]Stanley Hauerwas, *Matthew* (Grand Rapids: Brazos Press, 2006), 244.

[7]Iris Marion Young, *Justice and the Politics of Difference* (Princeton: Princeton University Press, 1990).

[8]Dixa Ramírez, "Salomé Ureña's Blurred Edges: Race, Gender, and Commemoration in the Dominican Republic." *The Black Scholar: Journal of Black Studies and Research.* Vol. 45, 2015, Issue 2: Dominican Black Studies, 45–56. Published online May 19, 2017. Accessed online April 2, 2018.

[9]Michal Beth Dinkler, "The Acts of the Apostles," in *The New Testament Fortress Commentary on the Bible.* Margaret Aymer, Cynthia Briggs Kittredge, and David A. Sánchez, editors. (Minneapolis: Fortress Press, 2014), 338–40.

[10]Clarice Martin, "A Chamberlain's Journey and the Challenge of Interpretation for Liberation" *Semeia* 47 (1989): 105–35.

[11]James Cone, *A Black Theology of Liberation* (Philadelphia: Lippincott, 1970), 121.

[12]Randolph Campbell, *An Empire for Slavery: The Peculiar Institution in Texas, 1821-1865* (Baton Rouge: Louisiana State University Press, 1989).

[13]Ibid. Campbell cites a letter Austin wrote May 30, 1833, when he traveled to Mexico City by way of Matamoros.

The Work Continues:
Select Bibliography

Many denominations have written policies, statements, or curriculum about anti-racism that can be made available to your congregation. Contact your local denominational office for the latest resources.

Selective Bibliography

Adams, Maurianne, et al. *Readings for Diversity and Social Justice: An Anthology on Racism, Antisemitism, Sexism, Heterosexism, Ableism, and Classism.* New York: Routledge, 2000.

Adichie, Chimamanda Ngozi. *Americanah.* New York: Anchor Books, 2014.

Ahmed, Sarah. "Declarations of Whiteness: The Non-Performativity of Anti-Racism," *borderlands,* vol. 3 no. 2 (2004), http://www.borderlands.net.au/vol3no2_2004/ahmed_declarations.htm

Alexander, Michelle. *The New Jim Crow: Mass Incarceration in the Age of Colorblindness.* New York: New Press, 2010.

Barndt, Joseph. *Becoming an Anti-Racist Church: Journeying Toward Wholeness.* Minneapolis: Augsburg Fortress Press, 2011.

Blount, Brian K., general ed.; Cain Hope Felder, Clarice Martin, and Emerson Powery, associate eds. *True to Our Native Land: An African American New Testament Commentary.* Minneapolis: Augsburg Fortress Press, 2007.

Bonilla-Silva, Eduardo. *Racism without Racists: Color-Blind Racism and the Persistence of Racial Inequality in America,* third ed. Lanham, Md.: Rowman & Littlefield Publishers, Inc., 2009.

Boyd, Drick. *White Allies in the Struggle for Racial Justice.* Maryknoll, N.Y.: Orbis Books, 2015.

Brock, Rita Nakashima. *Journeys by Heart: A Christology of Erotic Power.* New York: Crossroad, 1988.

Campbell, Randolph. *An Empire for Slavery: The Peculiar Institution in Texas, 1821-1865.* Baton Rouge: Louisiana State University Press, 1989.

Campt, David. *The White Ally Toolkit Workbook: Using Active Listening, Empathy, and Personal Storytelling to Promote Racial Equity.* 2018. Available online at https://www.whiteallytoolkit.com/

Carter, J. Kameron. *Race: A Theological Account.* New York: Oxford University Press, 2008.

Cheng, Anne Anlin. *The Melancholy of Race: Psychoanalysis, Assimilation, and Hidden Grief.* Oxford University Press, 2001.

Cheng, Patrick S. *Rainbow Theology: Bridging Race, Sexuality, and Spirit.* New York: Seabury Books, 2013.

Choi, Woosung Calvin, *Preaching to Multiethnic Congregation: Positive Marginality as a Homiletical Paradigm.* New York: Peter Lang Press, 2015.

Cone, James H. *Black Theology and Black Power.* New York: Seabury Press, 1969.

———. *The Cross and the Lynching Tree.* Maryknoll, N.Y.: Orbis, 2013.

Copeland, M. Shawn. *Enfleshing Freedom: Body, Race, and Being.* Minneapolis: Fortress Press, 2009.

DeYoung, Curtiss Paul, et al. *United by Faith: The Multiracial Congregation as an Answer to the Problem of Race.* New York: Oxford University Press, 2004.

Dyson, Michael Eric. *Tears We Cannot Stop: A Sermon to White America.* New York: St. Martin's Press, 2017.

Edwards, Korie L. *The Elusive Dream: The Power of Race in Interracial Churches.* Oxford, New York: Oxford University Press, 2008.

Ellison, Gregory C. II. *Cut Dead, But Still Alive: Caring for African American Young Men.* Nashville: Abingdon Press, 2013.

———. *Fearless Dialogues: A New Movement for Justice.* Louisville: Westminster John Knox Press, 2017.

Ellison, Ralph. *Invisible Man.* New York: Random House, 1952.

Emerson, Michael O., and Christian Smith, *Divided by Faith: Evangelical Religion and the Problem of Race in America.* New York: Oxford University Press, 2000.

Felder, Cain Hope, ed. *Stony the Road We Trod: African American Biblical Interpretation.* Minneapolis: Fortress Press, 1991.

Fry Brown, Teresa, *Weary Throats and New Songs: Black Women Proclaiming God's Word.* Nashville: Abingdon Press, 2003.

González, Justo L., and Pablo A. Jiménez, *Púlpito: An Introduction to Hispanic Preaching.* Nashville: Abingdon Press, 2005.

Hansen, David Phillips. *Native Americans, the Mainline Church, and the Quest for Interracial Justice.* St. Louis: Chalice Press, 2016.

Hartigan, John Jr. *Odd Tribes: Toward a Cultural Analysis of White People.* Durham, N.C.: Duke University Press, 2005.

Harvey, Jennifer. *Dear White Christians: For Those Still Longing for Racial Reconciliation.* Grand Rapids, Mich.: Eerdmans, 2014.

Harvey, Paul. *Bounds of Their Habitation: Race and Religion in American History.* Lanham, Md.: Rowman & Littlefield, 2017.

Helms, Janet. *Black and White Racial Identity: Theory, Research, and Practice.* New York: Greenwood Press, 1990.

Hurd, Michael. *Thursday Night Lights: The Story of Black High School Football in Texas.* Austin: University of Texas Press, 2017.

Isasi-Díaz, Ada María. *En La Lucha / In the Struggle: A Hispanic Woman's Liberation Theology.* Minneapolis: Augsburg Fortress Press, 1993.

———. *Mujerista Theology.* Maryknoll, N.Y.: Orbis Books, 1996.

Jennings, Willie James. *The Christian Imagination: Theology and the Origins of Race.* New Haven, Conn.: Yale University Press, 2010.

Jones, Serene. *Feminist Theory and Christian Theology: Cartographies of Grace.* Minneapolis: Fortress Press, 2000.

Kelsey, George D. *Racism and the Christian Understanding of Man.* New York: Scribner, 1965.

Kim, Eunjoo Mary. *Preaching the Presence of God: A Homiletic from an Asian American Perspective.* Valley Forge, Pa.: Judson Press, 1999.

———. *Women Preaching: Theology and Practice Through the Ages.* Eugene, Oreg.: Wipf & Stock, 2004.

LaRue, Cleophus *The Heart of Black Preaching.* Louisville: Westminster John Knox Press, 1999.

Long, Thomas G. *The Witness of Preaching,* third ed. Louisville: Westminster John Knox Press, 2016.

López, Ian Haney. *White by Law: The Legal Construction of Race.* New York: NYU Press, 206.

McIntosh, Peggy. "White Privilege: Unpacking the Invisible Knapsack," in Monica McGoldrick, ed., *Re-Visioning Family Therapy: Race, Culture, and Gender in Clinical Practice.* New York: Guilford Press, 1998.

Medina, José. *The Epistemology of Resistance: Gender and Racial Oppression, Epistemic Injustice, and Resistant Imaginations.* New York: Oxford University Press, 2012.

Ngo, Helen. *The Habits of Racism: A Phenomenology of Racism and Racialized Embodiment.* Lanham, Md: Lexington Books, 2017.

Omi, Michael, and Howard Winant. *Racial Formation in the United States: From the 1960s to the 1990s,* second ed. New York: Routledge, 1994.

Rah, Soong-Chan. *Many Colors: Cultural Intelligence for a Changing Church.* Chicago: Moody Press, 2010.

Ray, Stephen G. Jr. *Do No Harm: Social Sin and Christian Responsibility.* Minneapolis: Augsburg Fortress Press, 2003.

Richardson, Rick, "Cross-Cultural Preaching: How to Connect in Our Multicultural Word." In Haddon Robinson and Craig Brian Larson, eds., *The Art and Craft of Biblical Preaching.* Grand Rapids, Mich.: Zondervan, 2005.

Ricouer, Paul. *The Course of Recognition,* trans. David Pellauer. Cambridge, Mass.: Harvard University Press, 2007.

Robinson, Haddon, and Craig Brian Larson, eds. *The Art and Craft of Biblical Preaching.* Grand Rapids, Mich.: Zondervan, 2005.

Sanders, Cody, and Angela Yarber. *Microaggressions in Ministry: Confronting the Hidden Violence of Everyday Church.* Louisville: Westminster John Knox Press, 2015.

Salaita, Steven. *Anti-Arab Racism in the USA: Where It Comes from and What It Means for Politics.* London, U.K.: Pluto Press, 2006.

Silva, Kumarini. *Brown Threat: Identification in the Security State.* Minneapolis: University of Minnesota Press, 2016.

Smith, Christine M. *Preaching as Weeping, Confession, and Resistance: Radical Responses to Radical Evil.* Louisville: Westminster John Knox Press, 1992.

Tatum, Beverly Daniel. *"Why Are All the Black Kids Sitting Together in the Cafeteria?": And Other Conversations about Race.* New York: BasicBooks, 1997.

———. Talking about Race, Learning about Racism: The Application of Racial Identity Development Theory in the Classroom," *Harvard Educational Review* 62, no. 1 (1992).

Thomas, Frank A. *Introduction to the Practice of African American Preaching.* Nashville: Abingdon Press, 2016.

———. *How to Preach a Dangerous Sermon.* Nashville: Abingdon Press, 2018.

Tisdale, Leonora Tubbs. *Prophetic Preaching: A Pastoral Approach*. Louisville: Westminster John Knox Press, 2010.

West, Traci. *Disruptive Christian Ethics: When Racism and Women's Lives Matter*. Louisville: Westminster John Knox Press, 2006.

Williams, Delores S. *Sisters in the Wilderness: The Challenge of Womanist God-Talk*. Maryknoll, N.Y.: Orbis Books, 1993.

Willimon, William H. *Who Lynched Willie Earle? Preaching to Confront Racism*. Nashville: Abingdon Press, 2017.

Young, Iris Marion. *Justice and the Politics of Difference*. Princeton: Princeton University Press, 1990.

Acknowledgments

Thank you. I didn't write my "thank you" at the end of my first book, but my heart has been full of gratitude for the many people who have helped to make both *Anxious to Talk about It* and this second book possible. So allow me to make up for lost time by thanking all of the people who have helped me to get these two books out in 2018.

First, the wonderful people at Chalice Press. Brad Lyons, thank you for taking on this first-time author and convincing me as an academic that I had something to say to laypeople, and that I could write in a way that was accessible. Deborah Arca, thank you for pushing me beyond my comfort zone to get the word out about my book. Thanks to K.J. Reynolds, Gail Stobaugh, and Connie Wang for all of the behind-the-scenes work required to get a book published. And thanks to Mick Silva for editing both books so well!

A big thank you to Austin Seminary for encouraging its faculty to write for the church. Ted Wardlaw, our President, is a pastor with a heart committed to serving the church, and his leadership sets the tone for the rest of the faculty. To Candace Mathis, who did a tremendous job of reading and editing earlier versions. Thank you to all my colleagues who have been so supportive of me during my first three years of teaching: Margaret Aymer, Cindy Rigby, Jen Lord, Suzie Park, Asante Todd, Paul Hooker, Eric Wall, Timothy Lincoln, David White, Melissa Wiginton, Lewie Donelson, Bill Greenway, Whit Bodman, David Johnson, Gregory Cuellar, Phil Wingeier-Rayo, Blair Monie, David Jensen, and Phil Helsel. These colleagues and friends are named in no particular order and are all very dear to me.

Phil Helsel, in particular, though, is especially dear. Thank you, Phil, for your partnership in work, writing, and family life. Thanks for all the time you spent with the kids so I could go out of town to talk about my first book. Thanks for all the little and big ways you have helped me get this second book sent off to the publisher.

A deep gratitude for all my teachers and colleagues from Emory: my classmates Melva Sampson, Mark Jefferson, Jake Myers, Jan Rippentrop, Chris Holmes, and all the amazing professors who taught me while I was there: my advisor Tom Long, Teresa Fry Brown, Luke Timothy Johnson, Emmanuel Y. Lartey, Elizabeth Bounds, Vincent Lloyd, Ed Philips, and Pam Hall, to name just a few. Greg Ellison, who I never got to take a class from, but from whom I am constantly learning: thank you, dear friend.

Friends along the journey: Jessica Vasquez-Torres and Laura Cheifitz, thank you for putting up with me and letting me into your circle of coolness. Mihee Kim-Kort, thank you for being an inspiration through your own writing and an early voice that told me, "You can do this!" Jenelle Holmes and Sara Webb Philips, thank you for reading an early draft of this manuscript and giving me helpful feedback. Patrice Pryor, Berica Day Westbrook, and Katie Loftin, thank you for knowing me for 30 years and still loving me, and continuing to remind me how to have fun! Jen Hunt, thank you for suffering alongside me, and for shining your light wherever you go. To all my professors from seminary and college who continue to inspire me: thanks for modeling the power of education and Christian formation. To Sally Brown, Luke Powery, Dave Ward, Eunjoo Mary Kim, Donyelle McCray, Gerald Liu, Ted Smith, and all the other amazing professors of preaching in the Academy of Homiletics who have been my friends and conversation partners: thank you. I am grateful to Steve Miller, founder of the HBCU Truth and Reconciliation Oral History Project, for including me as a faculty advisor and enabling me to listen to the stories of so many who have shared their experiences with racial discrimination. To all of you who have told your story: thank you.

To my mom and dad, Jeanne and Robert Browning, for raising me in the church and showering me with love, along with my brother and sisters: Chris, Helen, Sarah, Catherine, and Eloise. Thank you to my home church, First Presbyterian Church of San Antonio, for first teaching me about the faith and exposing me to great preaching through the ministry of Louis Zbinden. Thank you to the church I attend in Austin, Westlake Hills Presbyterian Church, and my life group—Courtney and Andrew, Anne and Brad, Laura and Scott, Martin and Elizabeth, Charmaine and Dalton, Natalie and Shannon—for the way you all have walked with me and prayed for me as I tried to make deadlines. My heart is so full and grateful for you all.

Finally, to Caleb and Evelyn, and to the next generation who will continue to work toward a world that is more just and loving for all: thank you. Ultimately, I am grateful to the God who has led me thus far along the way, the Source of all good gifts. For all this, I give thanks.

Can the church help America emerge from its racist shadows empowered to heal our racial divides?

ISBN 9780827215122

Yes, says pastor, professor, and former police officer Terrell Carter. Carter examines the deep roots of racism in America and how it continues to be perpetuated today, and shares practical strategies for racial reconciliation through the creation of multicultural communities focused on relationship, listening, and learning from each other.

ChalicePress.com   800-366-3383

When there's so much conflict around the country and around the corner, it's easy to feel overwhelmed and helpless.

What can one person do to make a difference?

"This is a book to be cherished." —Eboo Patel

TRANSFORMING COMMUNITIES

How People Like You Are Healing Their Neighborhoods

Sandhya Rani Jha

ISBN 9780827237155

Take heart and be inspired by real stories of ordinary people who took action and changed their corner of the world, one block at a time. Equal parts inspiration, education, and do-it-yourself, *Transforming Communities* will open your eyes to the world-healing potential within you, and give you the vision, the tools, and the encouragement to start transforming *your* neighborhood.

ChalicePress.com   800-366-3383

"Michael W. Waters... is both blunt and lyrical as he meditates on police violence, racism, hip-hop, and the power of faith."
—*Sojourners*

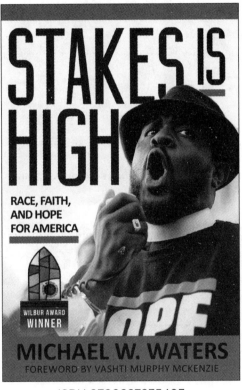

ISBN 9780827235403

Dallas pastor, community leader, and activist Michael Waters weaves stories of the past and present to create a sense of urgency for the need for racial justice in America today. Listen to the stories and join the work for justice.

Part of the Forum for Theological Exploration series.

ChalicePress.com   800-366-3383

Also by CAROLYN HELSEL

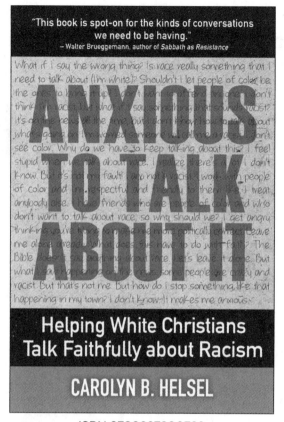

"This book is spot-on for the kinds of conversations we need to be having."
– Walter Brueggemann, author of *Sabbath as Resistance*

ANXIOUS TO TALK ABOUT IT

Helping White Christians Talk Faithfully about Racism

CAROLYN B. HELSEL

ISBN 9780827200722

Drawing from more than a decade of work with white congregations on race issues, professor and pastor Carolyn B. Helsel explores and engages the anxiety many Christians experience about racism and paves a way forward for more informed, compassionate, and healing conversations.

ChalicePress.com   800-366-3383